Microsoft Access 2000
explained

Books Available

By both authors:

BP327 DOS one step at a time
BP337 A Concise User's Guide to Lotus 1-2-3 for Windows
BP341 MS-DOS explained
BP346 Programming in Visual Basic for Windows
BP352 Excel 5 explained
BP362 Access one step at a time
BP387 Windows one step at a time
BP388 Why not personalise your PC
BP400 Windows 95 explained
BP406 MS Word 95 explained
BP407 Excel 95 explained
BP408 Access 95 one step at a time
BP409 MS Office 95 one step at a time
BP415 Using Netscape on the Internet*
BP420 E-mail on the Internet*
BP426 MS-Office 97 explained
BP428 MS-Word 97 explained
BP429 MS-Excel 97 explained
BP430 MS-Access 97 one step at a time
BP433 Your own Web site on the Internet
BP448 Lotus SmartSuite 97 explained
BP456 Windows 98 explained*
BP460 Using Microsoft Explorer 4 on the Internet*
BP464 E-mail and news with Outlook Express*
BP465 Lotus SmartSuite Millennium explained
BP471 Microsoft Office 2000 explained
BP472 Microsoft Word 2000 explained
BP473 Microsoft Excel 2000 explained
BP474 Microsoft Access 2000 explained
BP478 Microsoft Works 2000 explained

By Noel Kantaris:

BP258 Learning to Program in C
BP259 A Concise Introduction to UNIX*
BP284 Programming in QuickBASIC
BP325 A Concise User's Guide to Windows 3.1

Microsoft Access 2000 explained

by
P.R.M. Oliver
and
N. Kantaris

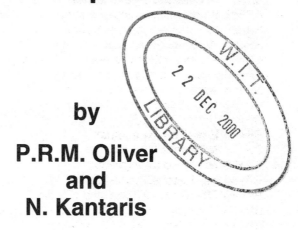

Bernard Babani (publishing) Ltd
The Grampians
Shepherds Bush Road
London W6 7NF
England

Please Note

Although every care has been taken with the production of this book to ensure that any projects, designs, modifications and/or programs, etc., contained herewith, operate in a correct and safe manner and also that any components specified are normally available in Great Britain, the Publishers and Author(s) do not accept responsibility in any way for the failure (including fault in design) of any project, design, modification or program to work correctly or to cause damage to any equipment that it may be connected to or used in conjunction with, or in respect of any other damage or injury that may be so caused, nor do the Publishers accept responsibility in any way for the failure to obtain specified components.

Notice is also given that if equipment that is still under warranty is modified in any way or used or connected with home-built equipment then that warranty may be void.

First Published - November 1999

British Library Cataloguing in Publication Data:

A catalogue record for this book is available from the British Library

ISBN 0 85934 474 6

Cover Design by Gregor Arthur
Cover illustration by Adam Willis
Printed and Bound in Great Britain by Cox & Wyman Ltd, Reading

About this Book

Microsoft Access 2000 explained has been written to help users to store and retrieve information using this latest Windows database from Microsoft. No previous knowledge of database design is assumed.

The book does not describe how to install Microsoft Windows 98 or higher, or how to set up your computer's hardware. If you need to know more about these topics, then may we suggest that you select an appropriate level book for your needs from the 'Books Available' list - the books are graduated in complexity with the less demanding *One step at a time* series, followed by the *Concise Introduction* series, to the more detailed *Explained* series. They are all published by BERNARD BABANI (publishing) Ltd.

In the first chapter, we give an overview of the database systems and we define the elements that make up an Access relational database management system. The hardware and software requirements of your system are also discussed, so that you know in advance the minimum system configuration for the successful installation and use of the package.

Below we list some of the major enhancements found in this latest version of Microsoft Access 2000:

- Redesigned online help and extended IntelliSense technology.

- New and improved Wizards, making it easy to create and maintain a number of common business and personal databases. There are Wizards to create just about anything you want.

- An Access database now supports record-level locking, in addition to page-level locking.

- You can now move freely between the Find and Replace dialogue boxes and the data.

- You can use the characters of any language that Unicode supports in your data, and easily work with the Euro symbol.

- Menus and toolbars are adjusted automatically as you work so that only the commands and toolbar buttons you use most often appear. There are many new toolbar features, and you can assign a hyperlink to a toolbar button or menu command for easy access to a location on your computer, a network, an intranet or the Internet.

- Many new features have been added to help you easily use the Internet, such as data access pages to add, edit, view, or manipulate current data in a Microsoft Access or SQL Server database.

The major features of the package (both old and new) are discussed using simple examples that the user is encouraged to type in, save, and modify as more advanced features are introduced. This provides the new user with an example that aims to help with the learning of the most commonly used features of the package, and should help to provide the confidence needed to tackle some of the more advanced features later.

This book was written with the busy person in mind. It is not necessary to learn all there is to know about a subject, when reading a few selected pages can usually do the same thing quite adequately!

With the help of this book, it is hoped that you will be able to come to terms with Microsoft Access 2000 and get the most out of your computer in terms of efficiency, productivity and enjoyment, and that you will be able to do it in the shortest, most effective and informative way.

If you would like to purchase a Companion Disc for any of the listed books by the same author(s), apart from the ones marked with an asterisk, containing the file/program listings which appear in them, then fill in the form at the back of the book and send it to Phil Oliver at the stipulated address.

About the Authors

Phil Oliver graduated in Mining Engineering at Camborne School of Mines in 1967 and since then has specialised in most aspects of surface mining technology, with a particular emphasis on computer related techniques. He has worked in Guyana, Canada, several Middle Eastern countries, South Africa and the United Kingdom, on such diverse projects as: the planning and management of bauxite, iron, gold and coal mines; rock excavation contracting in the UK; international mining equipment sales and international mine consulting for a major mining house in South Africa. In 1988 he took up a lecturing position at Camborne School of Mines (part of Exeter University) in Surface Mining and Management. He retired from full-time lecturing in 1998, to spend more time writing, consulting and developing Web sites for clients.

Noel Kantaris graduated in Electrical Engineering at Bristol University and after spending three years in the Electronics Industry in London, took up a Tutorship in Physics at the University of Queensland. Research interests in Ionospheric Physics, led to the degrees of M.E. in Electronics and Ph.D. in Physics. On return to the UK, he took up a Post-Doctoral Research Fellowship in Radio Physics at the University of Leicester, and then in 1973 a lecturing position in Engineering at the Camborne School of Mines, Cornwall, (part of Exeter University), where between 1978 and 1997 he was also the CSM Computing Manager. At present he is IT Director of FFC Ltd.

Acknowledgements

We would like to thank the staff of Text 100 Limited for providing the software programs on which this work was based.

Trademarks

Arial and **Times New Roman** are registered trademarks of The Monotype Corporation plc.

HP and LaserJet are registered trademarks of Hewlett Packard Corporation.

IBM is a registered trademark of International Business Machines, Inc.

Intel is a registered trademark of Intel Corporation.

Microsoft, **MS-DOS**, **Windows**, **Windows NT**, and **Visual Basic**, are either registered trademarks or trademarks of Microsoft Corporation.

PostScript is a registered trademark of Adobe Systems Incorporated.

TrueType is a registered trademark of Apple Corporation.

All other brand and product names used in the book are recognised as trademarks, or registered trademarks, of their respective companies.

Contents

1. **Package Overview** 1
   Hardware and Software Requirements 3
   Installing Access 4
   The Mouse Pointers 6

2. **Starting Access** 9
   Parts of the Access Screen 10
   The Menu Bar Options 13
   Shortcut Menus 17
   Using Help in Access 18
       The Help Toolbar 19
   The Office Assistant 20
       Customising the Office Assistant 22

3. **Database Basics** 25
   Database Elements 27
   An Instant Database 29
   The Database Window 31
       The Database Window Toolbar 32
   Creating Groups 33
   Sample Databases with Access 34
       Adding Access 2000 Features 34
       Some On-line Databases 36

4. **Creating Our Database** 37
   Opening a Database 37
   Creating a Table 37
       Data Types 40
   Sorting a Database Table 43
       Applying a Filter to a Sort 44
   Using a Database Form 45

Selecting Data 46
   Selecting Fields 46
   Selecting Records 46
   Selecting Cells 47
   Selecting Data in a Cell 47
   Zooming into a Cell 47
Working with Data 48
   Adding Records in a Table 48
   Finding Records in a Table 48
   Deleting Records from a Table 49
Manipulating Table Columns 50
   Adjusting Column Widths 50
   Hiding Fields 51
   Freezing Fields 51
   Moving a Field 52
   Inserting, Renaming and Deleting Fields 52
Adding a Lookup Column 53
   Editing a Lookup List 54
Printing a Table View 55

5.   Relational Database Design 57
Relationships 61
   Viewing and Editing Relationships 63
Creating an Additional Table 64

6.   Creating a Query 67
Types of Queries 70
The Query Window 71
   Creating a New Query 72
   Adding Fields to a Query Window 73
Types of Criteria 75
   Using Wildcard Characters in Criteria 75
Combining Criteria 76
Creating Calculated Fields 79
Using Functions in Criteria 80
   Finding Part of a Text Field 80
   Finding Part of a Date Field 81
   Calculating Totals in Queries 82

7. **More Advanced Queries** 85

   Types of Joins 87
   Creating a Parameter Query 88
   Creating a Crosstab Query 90
   Creating Queries for Updating Records 93
   Creating Action Queries 94
   Help on Queries 98

8. **Using Forms** 99

   Using the Form Wizard 100
       Creating a Form with a Subform 100
       Creating a Chart Form 104
   Customising a Form 106
   The Toolbox 108
   Adding a Combo Box 114
   Creating a Database Menu 117
       The Switchboard Manager 117
       An Autostart Menu 120

9. **Using Reports** 121

   The Report Wizard 122
   Types of Access Reports 125
   Report Views 125
   Help on Report Building 126
       The Northwind Database 127
   Sorting and Grouping Records 129
       Sorting Records 129
       Grouping Records 129
   Creating a Calculated Control 130
       Arithmetic Expressions 133
   Printing a Report 134

10. **Masking and Filtering Data** 135

   The Input Mask Property 135
   Importing or Linking Data 140
   Linked and Embedded Images 142

11. Access and the Internet 143
  Using Hypertext Links 143
      Creating a Hyperlink Field 144
      Inserting a Hyperlink 144
      Navigating the Internet from Access 145
  Creating Access Web Pages 146
      Static Web Pages 146
  Active Server Pages 147
      Requirements for ASP 147
      Exporting to an ASP File 147
  Data Access Pages 148
      Using the Page Wizard 148
      Viewing a Data Access Page 149
      Adding a Theme to a Page 150

12. Glossary of Terms 151

Index 171

1

Package Overview

Microsoft Access is a database management system (DBMS) designed to allow users to store, manipulate and retrieve information easily and quickly. A database is a collection of data that exists and is organised around a specific theme or requirement. It can be of the 'flat-file' type, or it can have relational capabilities, as in the case of Access, which is known as a relational database management system (RDBMS).

The main difference between flat-file and relational database systems is that the latter can store and manipulate data in multiple 'tables', while the former systems can only manipulate a single table at any given time. To make accessing the data easier, each row (or record) of data within a database table is structured in the same fashion, i.e., each record will have the same number of columns (or fields).

We define a database and its various elements as:

Database	A collection of data organised for a specific theme in one or more tables.
Table	A two-dimensional structure in which data is stored, like in a spreadsheet
Record	A row of information in a table relating to a single entry and comprising one or more fields.
Field	A single column of information of the same type, such as people's names.

In Access 2000 the maximum size of a database is 2 gigabyte and can include linked tables in other files. The

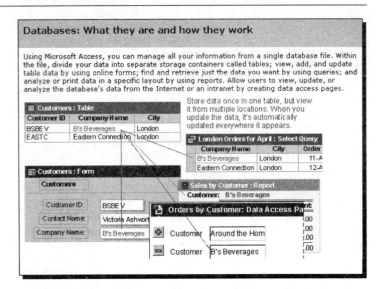

Databases: What they are and how they work

Using Microsoft Access, you can manage all your information from a single database file. Within the file, divide your data into separate storage containers called tables; view, add, and update table data by using online forms; find and retrieve just the data you want by using queries; and analyze or print data in a specific layout by using reports. Allow users to view, update, or analyze the database's data from the Internet or an intranet by creating data access pages.

number of objects in a database is limited to 32,768, while the maximum number of fields in a table is limited to 255.

A good example of a flat-file database would be the invoicing details kept on its clients by a company. These details could include name of client, description of work done, invoice number, and amount charged, something like the following:

NAME	Consultancy	Invoice	Value
VORTEX Co. Ltd	Wind Tunnel Tests	9701	120.84
AVON Construction	Adhesive Tests	9702	103.52
BARROWS Associates	Tunnel Design Tests	9703	99.32
STONEAGE Ltd	Carbon Dating Tests	9704	55.98
PARKWAY Gravel	Material Size Tests	9705	180.22
WESTWOOD Ltd	Load Bearing Tests	9706	68.52

Such a flat-file DBMS is too limited for the type of information normally held by most companies. If the same client asks for work to be carried out regularly, then the details for that client (which could include address, telephone and fax numbers, contact name, date of invoice, etc.), will have to be entered several times. This can lead to errors, but above all to redundant information being kept on a client, as each entry would have to have the name of the client, their address, telephone and fax numbers.

The relational facilities offered by Access, overcome the problems of entry errors and duplication of information. The ability to handle multiple tables at any one time allows for the grouping of data into sensible subsets. For example, one table, called client, could hold the names of the clients, their addresses, telephone and fax numbers, while another table, called invoice, could hold information on the work done, invoice number, date of issue, and amount charged. The two tables must, however, have one unique common field, such as a client reference number. The advantage is that details of each client are entered and stored only once, thus reducing the time and effort wasted on entering duplicate information, and also reducing the space required for data storage.

Hardware and Software Requirements

If Microsoft Access 2000 is already installed on your computer, you can safely skip this and the next section of this chapter.

If you currently run Access 97 on your PC with no compatibility problems, you shouldn't have too much trouble upgrading to Access 2000.

To install and use Access 2000, you need an IBM-compatible PC equipped with a Pentium 75 MHz or higher processor. In addition, you need the following:

- Windows 95/98 or later operating system, or Windows NT Workstation version 4.0 Service Pack 3 or later.

- Random access memory (RAM): 24MB, more recommended when running large databases.

- Hard disc space available for Access: 161MB, but this may vary depending on your configuration.

- Video adapter: VGA or higher resolution, Super VGA is recommended.

- A CD-ROM drive and a Microsoft compatible Mouse.

Realistically, to run Microsoft Access 2000 with reasonable sized databases, you will need a fast Pentium PC with at least 32MB of RAM. To run Access from a network, you must also have a network compatible with your Windows operating environment, such as Microsoft's Windows 98, Windows NT, LAN Manager, or Novell's NetWare.

Although it is possible to operate Microsoft Access from the keyboard, the availability of a mouse is essential. After all, pointing and clicking at an option on the screen to start an operation or command, is a lot easier than having to learn several different key combinations.

Installing Access

Installing Access on your computer's hard disc is made very easy with the SETUP program, which even configures Access automatically to take advantage of the computer's hardware and maintains any settings you had with a previous version.

Insert the program CD in the CD-ROM drive and with Windows 98 the SETUP program starts automatically. If this does not happen, do not panic (yet), it is easy to start manually.

- Click the Windows **Start** button and then click **Run**. Type:

  D:\setup.exe

  In the **Open** textbox and press return. If your CD-ROM drive has a letter other than D:, then obviously you would use that in the above command.

- SETUP will scan your system for already installed parts of Microsoft Office and will ask you for the key number on the back of the CD box.

- Follow the SETUP instructions, and when the dialogue box appears on the screen, similar to the one shown below, select the Access options you want to install.

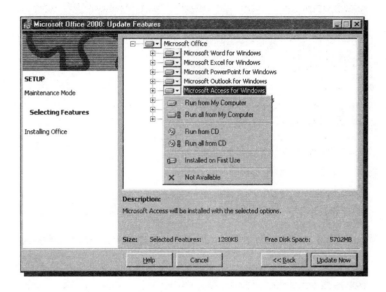

The SETUP program, or launcher as Microsoft call it, is the best we have seen yet. This is just as well as the default installation does not install everything you may need, and if you are not careful you will be coming back to the CD a few times in the future.

As shown above you can select to have items run from your computer, from the CD, or installed when needed. We suggest that if you have the disc space you select everything to **Run from My Computer**.

When all the files have been read, the SETUP program will modify your system files automatically so that you can start Access easily. It even detects your computer's processor and display, and configures Access to run smoothly with your system.

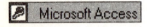 Finally, Access creates and displays a new entry in the Start, Programs cascade menu, with the new 2000 series icon shown here. Clicking this menu entry will start Microsoft Access. If you have MS-Office installed, SETUP also adds Access to the Microsoft Shortcut Bar facility, if you use it.

The Mouse Pointers

In Microsoft Access, as with all other graphical based programs, a mouse makes many operations both easier and 'more fun' to carry out.

Access makes use of the mouse pointers available in Windows, some of the most common of which are illustrated below. When Access is initially started up the first you will see is the hourglass, which turns into an upward pointing hollow arrow once the application screen appears on your display. Other shapes depend on the type of work you are doing at the time.

 The hourglass which displays when you are waiting while performing a function.

 The arrow which appears when the pointer is placed over menus, scrolling bars, buttons, and dialogue boxes.

 The I-beam which appears in normal text areas of the screen.

 The large 4-headed arrow which appears after choosing the Control, Move/Size command(s) for moving or sizing windows.

The double arrows which appear when over the border of a window, used to drag the side and alter the size of the window.

The Help hand which appears in the Help windows, and is used to access 'hypertext' type links.

Microsoft Access 2000, like the rest of the Microsoft Office applications and other Windows packages, has additional mouse pointers which facilitate the execution of selected commands. Some of these, shown below, have the following functions:

The vertical pointer which appears when pointing over a column in a table, used to select the column.

The horizontal pointer which appears when pointing at a row in a database table, used to select the row.

The slanted arrow which appears when the pointer is placed in the selection bar area of a database table.

The vertical split arrow which appears when pointing over the area separating two columns in a database table, used to size a column.

The horizontal split arrow which appears when pointing over the area separating two rows in a table, used to size a row.

The frame cross which you drag to create a frame while designing a Form.

Access has a few additional mouse pointers to the ones above, but their shapes are mostly self-evident.

Some Access windows display a '?' button, usually in the top right corner, next to the 'X' close button, as shown here. Clicking this button changes the mouse pointer from its usual inclined arrow shape to the 'What's this?' shape. Pointing to an object in the dialogue box, menu or window and clicking with this, gives additional information on the object.

2

Starting Access

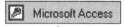 Access is started in Windows either by clicking the Taskbar **Start** button then selecting **Programs** and clicking on the 'Microsoft Access' icon on the cascade menu; by clicking the Access icon on the Microsoft Office Shortcut Bar; or by double-clicking on the icon of an Access database file. In the latter case the database will be loaded into Access at the same time.

When you start the Access program itself, the following dialogue box is displayed on your screen:

 From this box, you can either **Open an existing file**, or create a new one. If you elect to create a new database, then you can select either to create a **Blank Access database**, or use the **Access database wizards, pages and projects** option to help you with the creation of the new database.

Access 2000 makes extensive use of Wizards, which have been designed to help the new user to create databases more easily. In particular, the Database Wizard builds the necessary elements for over 20 different databases for both home and business use. All you have to do is to answer a set of questions and the Wizard builds the database for you.

Parts of the Access Screen

Before we start designing a database, let us take a look at a typical Access 2000 opening screen.

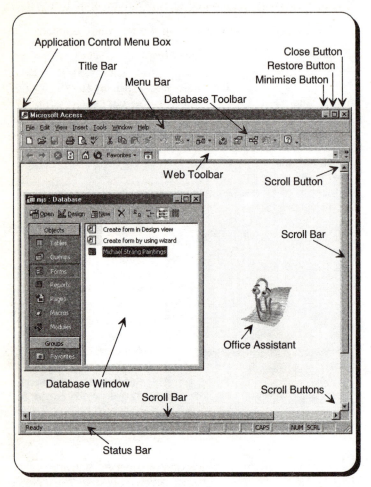

As you can see, these windows have common screen elements with those of other Microsoft Office applications. As usual, depending on what you are doing with Access, the items on the menu bar can be different from those of the opening screen. Although more than one window can be displayed simultaneously, only one is the active window (which normally displays on top of any other non-active windows. Title bars of non-active windows appear a lighter shade than those of the active one. To activate another window, click with the left mouse button anywhere within it.

The various screen areas have the following functions:

Area	*Function*
Command button	Clicking on this button, (see upper-left corner of the Access window), displays a pull-down menu which can be used to control the program window. It includes commands for restoring, moving, sizing, maximising, minimising, and closing the window.
Title bar	The bar at the top of a window which displays the application name.
Minimise box	When clicked, this button minimises the application to the Windows Taskbar.
Restore button	Clicking on this button restores the active window to the position and size that was occupied before it was maximised.
	The Restore button is then replaced by a Maximise button, shown here, which can then be used to set the window to full screen size.

Close button	The extreme top right button that you click to close a window.
Menu bar	The bar below the Title bar which allows you to choose from several menu options. Clicking on a menu item displays the pull-down menu associated with that item. The options listed in the Menu bar depend on what you are doing at the time, as well as your recent activities.
Toolbars	The bars below the Menu bar which contain buttons that give you mouse click access to the most often used functions in the program, as well as to Internet Web sites from within Access
Scroll Buttons	The arrowheads at each end of each scroll bar which you click to scroll the screen up and down one line, or left and right 10% of the screen, at a time.
Scroll Bars	The areas on the screen (extreme right and bottom of each window) that contain scroll boxes in vertical and horizontal bars. Clicking on these bars allows you to reach the part of the window that might not be visible on the screen.
Database Window	The control window for the currently open database.
Office Assistant	An 'automated' source of help on Access and database features.

Status Bar   The bottom line of the window that
                              displays status and other useful
                              information.

The Menu Bar Options

Each window's menu bar option has associated with it a
pull-down sub-menu. To activate the menu of a window,
either press the <Alt> key, which causes the first option of
the menu (in this case **File**) to be highlighted, then use the
right and left arrow keys to highlight any of the options in the
menu, or use the mouse to point to an option. Pressing either
the <Enter> key, or the left mouse button, reveals the
pull-down sub-menu of the highlighted menu option.

The sub-menu of the **File** option of the Access window, is
shown below.

Menu options can also be
activated directly by pressing the
<Alt> key followed by the
underlined letter of the required
option. Thus pressing **Alt+F**,
causes the pull-down sub-menu
of **File** to be displayed.

You can use the up and down
arrow keys to move the
highlighted bar up and down a
sub-menu, or the right and left
arrow keys to move along the
options in the menu bar. Pressing
the <Enter> key selects the
highlighted option or executes the
highlighted command. Pressing
the <Esc> key once, closes the
pull-down sub-menu, while
pressing the <Esc> key for a
second time, closes the menu
system.

Depending on what you are doing with Access, different sub-menu options are available or become active. Access 2000 also automatically personalises both menus and toolbars based on how often you use particular commands. When you first start the program, the most basic commands appear. Then, as you work, Access adjusts the menus and toolbars so that only the commands and toolbar buttons you use most often appear. To find a command you don't use often, or have never used before, click the arrows at the bottom of the menu to expand it to show all the options available, as shown below.

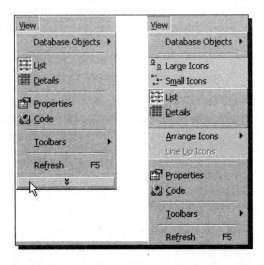

This shows the 'default' **View** menu on the left, and the same menu fully expanded on the right. The previously hidden options appearing in a lighter shade of grey.

You can also double-click the menu to expand it. When you expand one menu, all of the other menus are also expanded until you choose a command or perform another action.

When you click a command on the expanded menu, it is immediately added to the personalised menu. It is dropped from the personalised menu again if you use Access several times without using that command.

In general, Access 2000 menu options offer the following:

File Produces a pull-down menu of mainly file related tasks, such as creating a **New** database, the ability to **Open**, or **Close** database files, to **Get External Data** from other databases, and **Save** database files with the same name, or **Save As** a different name, or to **Export** into different file formats. You can use **Page Setup** to set the margins and the size of your printed page, **Print Preview** a table, form, or query on screen before committing it to paper, or **Print** it to paper. You can view **Database Properties**, and use the **Send To** option to attach a particular database feature to an e-mail. Finally, you can **Exit** the program. Above this last sub-menu option, Access also displays the last four databases you used so that you can open them easily.

Edit Produces a pull-down menu which allows you to **Undo** changes made, **Cut**, **Copy** and **Paste** text, and **Delete** or **Rename** a database object. When a database object is open additional options become available, with a table or a query for example, the abilities to select and delete columns or records, to **Find** or **Replace** specific text in the opened item, to **Go To** another record, or view and update **OLE/DDE Links**.

View This menu, shown on the previous page, gives you control over what you see on the screen. For example, you can choose to view several database objects, such as tables, queries, forms, etc., and view files as icons or lists. You can also select which toolbars you want to be displayed.

Insert   Allows you to insert tables, queries, forms, reports, pages, macros, or modules. You can even use **AutoForm** and **AutoReport** to create forms and reports automatically.

Tools   Allows you to spell-check your work, switch on the AutoCorrect facility, use Office links, or open a Microsoft Netmeeting. You can also add or change relationships between database tables, analyse features of your database, use an extensive range of utilities, specify the level of security required, run or create Visual Basic macros, customise the way Access operates for you and generally control its option settings.

Window   Allows you to display multiple windows on the screen in 'cascade' or 'tile' form, to arrange icons within an active window, or to hide or redisplay the active window.

Help   Activates the help menu which you can use to access **Microsoft Access Help**, to display the Office Assistant, to use the **What's This**? facility described below, or the **Office on the Web** option (if you are connected to the Internet). You can **Detect and Repair** some Access problems, or use the **About Microsoft Access** option to get details of your version of Access and your operating system.

For a more detailed description of each sub-menu item, click **What's This** on the **Help** menu and the pointer will change to a question mark. Clicking with this on the menu item you want information about opens a small text box of help.

When an object, such as a table, is open, additional menu options are displayed. With a table for example, the **Format** and **Records** menu options are available.

Shortcut Menus

To see a shortcut menu containing the most common commands applicable to an item, point with your mouse at the item and click the right mouse button. For example, left-clicking the adjacent Open Database icon, displays the Open dialogue box. Right-clicking within the file list area of this dialogue box, displays the short-cut menu shown below, with the following options:

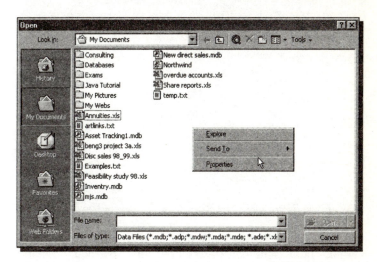

In this case we have the option to **Explore** the contents of the logged folder (My Documents), use the **Send To** option to send the contents of the folder to a variety of places such as the 3½" Floppy drive, or the Briefcase, (depending on your setup), or see the folder's **Properties**.

Having activated a shortcut menu, you can close it without taking any further action by simply pressing the <Esc> key.

If you do not use these shortcut menus we strongly recommend you start, as they can save you a lot of time.

Using Help in Access

The first time you start Access, it might be a good idea to look at the help available to you. To do this, cancel the opening dialogue box, then press the **F1** key and click the **Contents** tab to show the following Help screen.

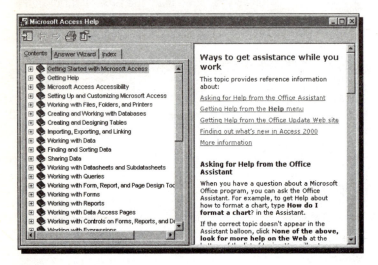

We suggest you spend a little time here browsing through the various help screens, particularly the first two; 'Getting Started with Microsoft Access' and 'Getting Help'. There are

several ways of using the above Help window. The **Contents** tab lets you scroll through a table of contents for Access Help. Clicking a '+' at the left of an item opens a sub-list, clicking a '-' will close it again. Clicking a list item, with the mark 🔲 as shown, opens the help text in the right-hand window.

To type a question in the Help window, you click the **Answer Wizard** tab. When you want to search for specific words or phrases, you click the **Index** tab.

For example, click the **A̲nswer Wizard** tab, and type the text *design a new database* in the **W̲hat would you like to do?** text box. Then click the **S̲earch** button and you should see something like the following.

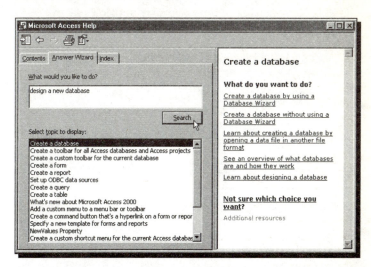

The right window offers help on several different aspects of creating databases. Have a look at them, at this stage most of them should be very useful.

The Help Toolbar

You can control the Help window with the five buttons on the toolbar, as follows:

Hide - Closes and re-opens the left half of the Help window, giving more room for the Help text.

Back - Opens the last Help page viewed in the current session list.

Forward - Opens the next Help page viewed in the current session list.

Print - prints either the current page, or all of the topics in the selected heading.

 Options - gives a sub-menu of all the other toolbar options, as well as allowing you to hide the Help tabs.

The Access Help system is very comprehensive but it is not always easy to find the information you are looking for. It usually pays to select the feature, or object, you want details on before accessing Help.

The Office Assistant

In an attempt to make the Help system more 'user friendly' Microsoft added the Office Assistant to the last version of Office. It has not changed very much in version 2000. It is a central source of information, and can be used from all the Office applications. So no matter which Office application you are using the Assistant is there to help you.

To find out how it works, use the **Help**, **Show the Office Assistant** menu command, or click the Access Help button, shown here. This last method, however, does not always open the Office Assistant, depending on how you have used Access in the recent past. Type the word *help* in the displayed 'What would you like to do?' box, shown to the left, and left-click the **Search** button.

A list of help topics is then displayed, as shown on the next page. To see more topics, left-click the small triangle at the bottom of this list.

To find out how you can use the Office Assistant and Help generally, click the 'Ways to get assistance while you work' option and work your way through the Help options offered.

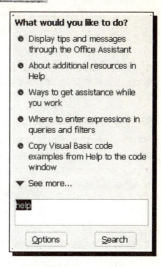

What would you like to do?

- Display tips and messages through the Office Assistant
- About additional resources in Help
- Ways to get assistance while you work
- Where to enter expressions in queries and filters
- Copy Visual Basic code examples from Help to the code window
- ▼ See more...

help

Options   Search

Next, try the option 'Display tips and messages through the Office Assistant' which opens the help window shown below. This shows you how to hide, show or turn off the Office Assistant, how to turn on or off automatic display of Help topics by the Assistant, how to display alert messages and also how to show a Tip of the Day when Access starts up.

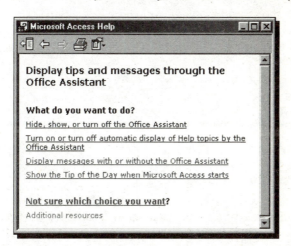

Microsoft Access Help

Display tips and messages through the Office Assistant

What do you want to do?

Hide, show, or turn off the Office Assistant

Turn on or turn off automatic display of Help topics by the Office Assistant

Display messages with or without the Office Assistant

Show the Tip of the Day when Microsoft Access starts

Not sure which choice you want?

Additional resources

From these few Help pages you should be able to find out almost anything you want to know about the Office Assistant.

Customising the Office Assistant

You can customise the Office Assistant to a great degree. Not only can you change the way it responds to your enquiries, but you can even switch it off once you have mastered a particular Office application.

To see the default options settings of the Office Assistant, activate it, left-click on it, and left-click the **Options** button on the displayed box. Doing this, opens the following dialogue box:

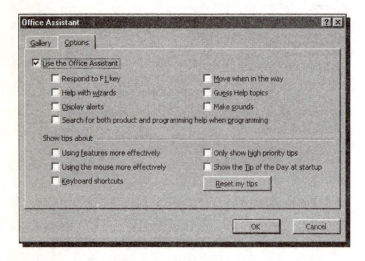

As you can see, it is possible to set a whole range of options. If you never want to use the Assistant, simply de-select the **Use the Office Assistant** option.

Should you want to change the shape of your Office Assistant (there are eight shapes to choose from - see next page), either left-click the Gallery tab of the above dialogue box, or right-click the Office Assistant and select the **Choose Assistant** option from the shortcut menu, as shown here.

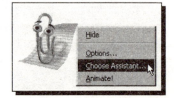

Either of these actions displays the following dialogue box, in which you can select your preferred Assistant shape by left-clicking the **Next** button, followed by **OK**.

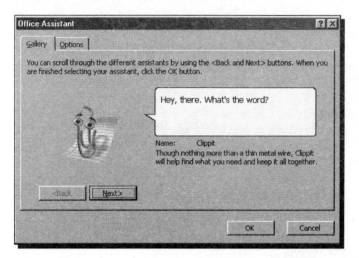

The shapes of the available Assistants are as follows:

The Assistant is very entertaining to watch, especially when the **Animate** option has been selected. We must admit though that we prefer to use Access, and the other Office applications with the Office Assistant turned off. It can get quite distracting! Obviously the choice is yours, but make sure you explore its features before turning the Assistant off.

3

Database Basics

Before we start designing a database using Access 2000, it would be a good idea to look at the various elements that make up a database. To do so, start Access, which opens the Microsoft Access dialogue box shown here. Next, select the **Blank Access database** option and click **OK**. Alternatively, you could

click the New Database toolbar icon, or use the **File, New** command, as all of these methods will open the New dialogue box shown below - with the General tab activated.

To create a new database, select the Database icon and press the **OK** button. This opens the File New Database dialogue box for you to name and save the database file.

In the **File name** box, type the database name, **Adept 1** is the sample database we will be building in the next chapter, so we will use that name. We suggest you go along with us to fully benefit from the example. The new name then replaces the default name **db1**. Access adds the extension **.mdb** automatically which, however, you don't have to worry too much about. In our example we are saving the new database in the My Documents folder on our C: drive, but you can obviously save it wherever you like. The Places Bar, shown in the left of the box above lets you quickly access many commonly used folders.

Finally, pressing the **Create** button creates the empty database and displays its Database window, as shown on the next page.

It is in this window that you can design the various elements that make up a database, such as tables, queries, forms, reports, pages, macros and modules, most of which we will examine in more detail in the rest of the book. The objects you add will appear in the Database window, so that you can select them and work with them.

Database Elements

The **Objects** area above displays the types of objects available in an Access 2000 database, these are:

▦ Tables
As we saw earlier, a table consists of fields and records of data, and is a collection of related information similar to a small spreadsheet. You must have at least one table in a database, but you can have many more.

▦ Queries
Queries allow you to find the information you want from your database. A query is set up to find the data that meets a specific set of criteria, or conditions.

▦ Forms
Forms usually display one record at a time, and provide an easy, more visual, way to view, enter and edit the information in that record.

Reports

Reports are formatted documents that display specific information from the database. Calculations and summaries are often carried out in reports.

Pages

Pages let you put 'live' database information onto the Internet, or your company's Intranet. Other users can then access and modify the data.

Macros

Macros can help you to automate tasks that you perform frequently. They combine a series of actions (that each perform a particular operation) into one action, such as clicking a macro button. They can save a lot of time.

Modules

Modules are programs created in Visual Basic for Applications (VBA) that let you control how your database works.

To get a first look at some of these objects we need an actual database that contains them. This is no problem with Access 2000, as you can use the Database Wizard to create a number of 'standard' types of databases. You simply choose the type that is suitable for the information you want to put in it. The Wizard then creates the new database, giving you options for customising it during the process, as we shall see in the next chapter.

For now we will simply create one of their standard databases to have something to play with, and to get a general idea about the workings of the Access package.

An Instant Database

If necessary, start Access 2000, select the **Access database wizards, pages and projects** option in the Microsoft Access dialogue box and click **OK**, to open the following:

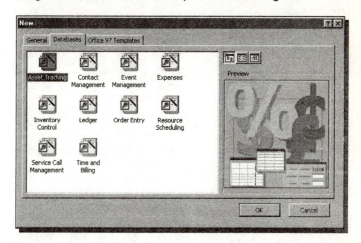

The New dialogue box shown above, can also be accessed from the New Database toolbar icon, or by using the **File, New** command; but with these you have to move to the Databases tab as shown above. The ten Access databases available to you are listed here. All of these are business orientated, but there are some personal ones hidden away, as we shall see at the end of the chapter.

Select the Asset Tracking icon and click the **OK** button to start the procedure. Select the default name *Asset Tracking1.mdb,* unless you prefer something else, and click the **Create** button in the File New Database dialogue box. This generates an empty Database window and opens the Database Wizard, as shown at the top of the next page.

After reading about the type of database that will be created, you have two choices. Clicking the **Next** button will step you through the Wizard, giving you customisation choices, while clicking the **Finish** button will create a database containing all the default elements.

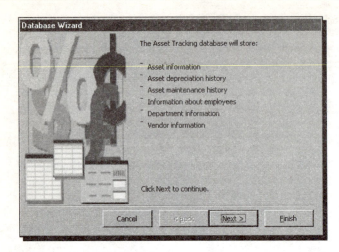

For now, select **Finish** and wait for a couple of minutes while the new database objects are created. The Database window

will then be reduced to an icon at the bottom of the screen, as shown on the left, and the opening Main Switchboard window of the database will display. This is simply a menu of database options, and is actually one of the database forms.

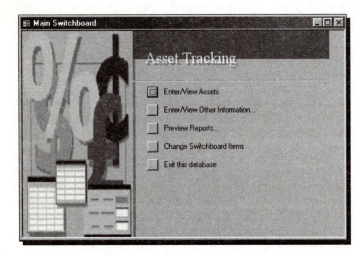

The Database Window

 When you are ready, restore the Database window, by double-clicking on its minimised icon, by clicking the Database Window toolbar button shown here, or by pressing the **F11** key. It should look something like that below.

Here 'Tables' is selected in the **Objects** bar, (or list), and the seven tables that make up this standard database are listed in the right-hand window pane. Selecting any of these and clicking the **Open** toolbar button will open that table, but there will not be any data in it. The whole database is empty, but it is ready to receive data.

Clicking the other Objects buttons in turn will show that there are also eleven forms, five reports and one module of code making up the database.

There are also options in each objects pane to start the procedure of creating a new object, such as 'Create table in Design view, by using wizard, or by entering data'. We shall see more of these procedures later.

The Database Window Toolbar

The buttons on this toolbar can save you a lot of time, so it is worth knowing their functions.

 Opens the selected object in a view that lets you work with data. This is the same as double-clicking the object.

 Opens the selected object in design view in which you can change the design and layout of the object.

 Starts the procedure for creating a new object of the type selected.

 Deletes the selected object, as long as it is not 'related' to another database object.

 Displays objects as large icons.

 Displays objects as small icons.

 Displays objects in a list format - the display type we usually use.

 Displays extra details in the objects list.

You can change the design of any of the objects, or elements, of a database by selecting them and clicking the **Design** toolbar button shown above.

This is a good place to experiment a little with the objects of this 'trial' database, as you can always delete the database and start again if you come to grief!

Creating Groups

To make it easier to use a database you can create groups in which to keep related objects in the Database window. This way you could, for example, keep all the tables, forms and reports dealing with the same type of data in the same objects window pane.

To create a group, click the Groups bar in the **Objects** list, right-click in the area below, select **New Group** and name the group. When you want to add an object to the group, simply drag it from the right pane of the database window to the group name in the objects list. A very useful feature.

In our example above we have created a group to hold the tables, forms and reports relating to 'Maintenance', but as you can see, we did not bother to rename it.

We also show above the shortcut menu that is opened when a Group button is right-clicked. Towards the bottom, this menu has three Group-related functions, including **Rename Group** and **Delete Group**.

Sample Databases with Access

Four sample databases were included with our version of Office 2000. These are all well worth looking at to see how they have been constructed. You may well be able to modify them to your actual needs, or use parts of them at least.

- The Northwind database contains the sales data for a company called Northwind Traders, which imports and exports speciality foods from around the world.

- Address Book - Use this application to manage addresses and other information for individuals, families, and companies.

- Contact Management - Use this application to manage your personal and business contacts.

- Household Inventory - Use this application to keep track of important possessions in your home.

If these were installed on your PC with Access you can easily find them from the Microsoft Access dialogue box (see page 25). Select **Open an existing file** and look in the list presented, if necessary clicking the 'More Files' option at the top of the list.

Adding Access 2000 Features

If these sample databases were not installed there is no problem as long as you have the CD-ROMs that were used for the original installation. If not, you will have to find them!

Place Disc 1 in your CD-ROM drive and open the Windows Control Panel by selecting **Start**, **Settings**, **Control Panel**. Then double-click the Add/Remove Programs icon to open the dialogue box shown on the next page.

Select the entry for your version of the program; in our case this was Microsoft Office 2000 Premium, but yours may be different, and click the **Add/Remove** button.

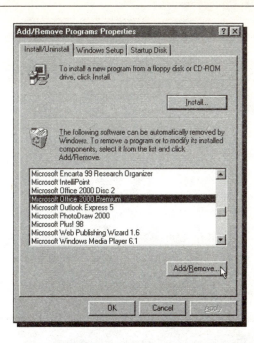

This opens the Office 2000 Maintenance Mode dialogue box shown below. Click the **Add or Remove Features** button

and open the Microsoft Access for Windows list in the Update Features box, as shown here.

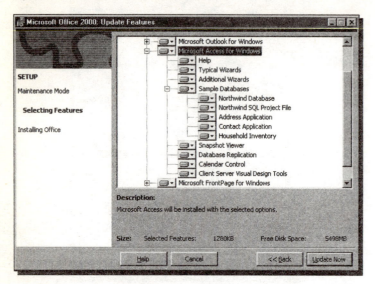

To install the sample databases, right-click the icon to the left of each one in turn and select **Run from my Computer** from the Shortcut menu. When all the Sample Database icons look like ours above simply click the **Update Now** button to install them on your machine.

Some On-line Databases

Microsoft have also placed some other databases and add-ins on their Web site. To access these, connect to the Internet, and use the following URL address in your browser:

```
Http://officeupdate.microsoft.com/downloadCatalog/
dldAccess.htm
```

Make sure you type it exactly the same as above, but all on one line and with no spaces. Hopefully you may find something of use there that you can download.

4

Creating Our Database

Opening a Database

We will now get to grips with developing the database that we created and named **Adept 1** in the last chapter. Start Access and select the option **Open an existing file** as shown here to the right.

Select the empty database **Adept 1** and press the **OK** button. If you did not create this file before, just go back to the beginning of the previous chapter and do it now. It will only take a minute or two, and you will need it to benefit from what we will be doing.

Creating a Table

The easiest way to design a database table is by double-clicking the **Create table by using wizard** button in the Database window as shown here, which opens the Table Wizard dialogue box. The other options on

the list, allow you to start designing a table from scratch in design view, or to have a table automatically created for you depending on the data you enter into it.

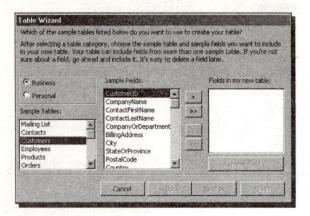

The database we are going to create holds the invoicing details which the firm Adept Consultants keep on their clients. One table will hold the details of the clients, while another will hold the actual invoice details.

The wizard helps you very rapidly create a whole range of tables suitable for business or personal databases - we counted 45 in fact.

With **Business** checked, choose 'Customers' from the **Sample Tables** list of the Table Wizard dialogue box, to reveal a list of appropriate fields for that table, as shown above.

You can either select all the fields with the >> button, or you can select a few. For our example, we selected the following fields: CustomerID, CompanyName, BillingAddress, City, StateOrProvince, PostalCode, ContactTitle, PhoneNumber, FaxNumber and Notes, by highlighting each in turn and pressing the > button.

Don't worry if these field names are not exactly what you want, as they can be easily changed. To change field names, highlight them in turn in the 'Fields in my new table' list and click the **Rename Field** button to reveal the Rename field dialogue box shown here.

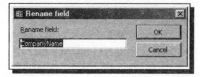

We suggest you change the selected field names to those listed below.

CompanyName	Name
BillingAddress	Address
City	Town
CustomerID	CustomerID
StateOrProvince	County
PostalCode	PostCode
ContactTitle	Contact
PhoneNumber	Phone
FaxNumber	Fax
Notes	Order

When you have completed renaming the field names, press the **Finish** button, which displays the Customers Table in Datasheet view ready for you to enter information, as shown below.

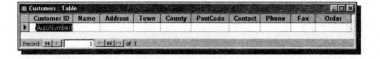

From this view, to redesign the table, including changing its field names, click the Design View icon shown here, or use the **View, Design View** main menu command. The table is then displayed in Design view.

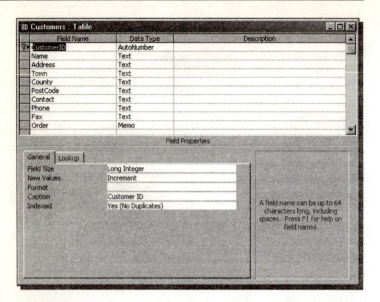

In Design view you can change the data type and properties of the fields in the table and give each one a description which is then displayed when that field is used in the database.

As each field name is highlighted, a Field Properties box appears at the bottom of the screen. If you were using this Design view to rename fields, then you should also edit the name appearing against the Caption property, or remove it altogether.

Data Types

Next, place the cursor at the end of the Data Type descriptor of the CustomerID field and click the down-arrow button which appears. This displays a drop-down list of data types, as shown here and explained overleaf.

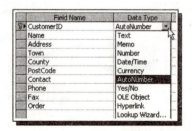

Data Type	Usage	Size
Text	Alphanumeric data	< 255 characters
Memo	Alphanumeric data, sentences and paragraphs	< 64,000 characters
Number	Numeric data	1, 2, 4, or 8 bytes (16 bytes for ReplicationID or Decimal)
Date/Time	Dates and times	8 bytes
Currency	Monetary values, stored with 4 decimal places of precision	8 bytes
AutoNumber	Unique value generated by Access for each new record	4 bytes (16 bytes for ReplicationID)
Yes/No	Boolean (true/false) data	<1 byte>
OLE Object	Pictures, graphs, or other ActiveX objects from other Windows-based applications	< about 1 gigabyte
Hyperlink	A link "address" to a document or file on the Web, an intranet, or on a local area network.	< 2048 characters

As we intend to use the first four letters of a company's name as the CustomerID field in our database, change its current data type from Autonumber to Text. Then save the table by clicking the Save button, before changing the data type of the last field (Order) from Memo to AutoNumber.

Finally, place the cursor against the Phone and Fax fields and delete the entry against the Input Mask in the Field Properties box. The type of input mask displayed here is ideal for USA Phone and Fax numbers, but it does not correspond to the entry form usually adopted in the UK, so it is best removed.

Click the Save icon again, or use the **File, Save** command to save your design changes, then click the Datasheet View icon (or use the **View, Datasheet View** command) to revert to the Customers table so that you can start entering the information below.

Customer ID	Name	Address	Town	County	Post Code	Contact
VORT	VORTEX Co. Ltd	Windy House	St. Austell	Cornwall	TR18 1FX	Brian Storm
AVON	AVON Construction	Riverside House	Stratford-on-Avon	Warwickshire	AV15 2QW	John Waters
BARR	BARROWS Associates	Barrows House	Bodmin	Cornwall	PL22 1XE	Mandy Brown
STON	STONEAGE Ltd	Data House	Salisbury	Wiltshire	SB44 1BN	Mike Irons
PARK	PARKWAY Gravel	Aggregate House	Bristol	Avon	BS55 2ZX	James Stone
WEST	WESTWOOD Ltd	Weight House	Plymouth	Devon	PL22 1AA	Mary Slim
GLOW	GLOWORM Ltd	Light House	Brighton	Sussex	BR87 4DD	Peter Summers
SILV	SILVERSMITH Co	Radiation House	Exeter	Devon	EX28 1PL	Adam Smith
WORM	WORMGLAZE Ltd	Glass House	Winchester	Hampshire	WN23 5TR	Richard Glazer
EALI	EALING Engines Design	Engine House	Taunton	Somerset	TN17 3RT	Trevor Miles
HIRE	HIRE Service Equipment	Network House	Bath	Avon	BA76 3WE	Nicole Webb
EURO	EUROBASE Co. Ltd	Control House	Penzance	Cornwall	TR15 8LK	Sarah Star

The widths of the above fields were changed so that all fields could be visible on the screen at the same time. To change the width of a field, place the cursor on the column separator until the cursor changes to the vertical split arrow, then drag the column separator to the right or left, to increase or decrease the width of the field.

For other methods of changing the widths of columns see the section later in this chapter.

Sorting a Database Table

As you enter information into a database table, you might elect to change the field headings by clicking the Design Table icon and editing a field name, say from Name to CompanyName. If you do this, when you return to the table in Datasheet view you will find that the records have sorted automatically in ascending order of the entries of the field in which you left the cursor while in Design view.

Contact	Phone	Fax	Order
Brian Storm	01776-223344	01776-224466	1
John Waters	01657-113355	01657-221133	2
Mandy Brown	01554-664422	01554-663311	3
Mike Irons	01765-234567	01765-232332	4
James Stone	01534-987654	01534-984567	5
Mary Slim	01234-667755	01234-669988	6
Peter Summers	01432-746523	01432-742266	7
Adam Smith	01336-997755	01336-996644	8
Richard Glazer	01123-654321	01123-651234	9
Trevor Miles	01336-010107	01336-010109	10
Nicole Webb	01875-558822	01875-552288	11
Sarah Star	01736-098765	01736-098567	12
			(AutoNumber)

If you want to preserve the order in which you entered your data, then sort by the last field (Order) with its type as AutoNumber. This can be done at any time, even after you finished entering all other information.

Sorting a database table in ascending order of an AutoNumber type field, results in the database table displaying in the order in which the data was originally entered in that table. Above, we show the Contact field, so that you can cross-check the original order of your Customer table, as well as the rest of the information in that table not shown in the screen dump of the previous page.

To sort a database table in ascending or descending order of the entries of any field, place the cursor in the required field and click the Sort Ascending or Sort Descending icon, shown here.

With the keyboard, select the **Records, Sort** command, then choose either the **Sort Ascending** or the **Sort Descending** option.

Applying a Filter to a Sort

If you would like to sort and display only records that fit selected criteria, use the **Records, Filter, Advanced Filter/Sort** command, which opens the Filter dialogue box, shown below.

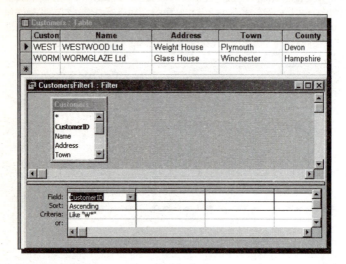

The upper portion of the dialogue box displays all the fields in the Customers table, while the lower portion is where you enter your filter restrictions.

In our example above, we chose to view, in ascending order, the records within the CustomersID field that start with W - we typed W* and Access displayed *Like "W*"*.

 When the Apply Filter icon, shown here, is pressed the Customers table displays with only two entries, as seen in the above composite screen dump. To go back to the display of all the records, click the same icon again, which now appears on the Toolbar depressed, and bears the name Remove Filter.

Using a Database Form

Once a table has been selected from the Database window, clicking the down-arrow against the New Object button and selecting **AutoForm**, automatically displays each record of that table in form view. The created form for the Customers table is shown below.

Forms can be used to enter, change or view data. They are mainly used to improve the way in which data is displayed on the screen.

Forms can also be used to sort records in a database table in descending or ascending order of a selected field.

When you attempt to close a new **Form** window, you will be asked if you would like to save it. An Access database can have

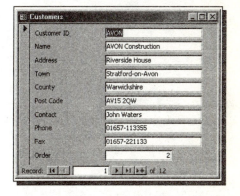

lots of different forms, each designed with a different purpose in mind. Saved forms are displayed in the Database window when you click the Forms object button. In the above example, we chose the default name suggested by Access, which was Customers.

In a later chapter we will discuss Forms and their design in some detail, including their customisation, but before we go any further we will now spend a little time looking at easy ways to manipulate the data in an Access database.

Selecting Data

As with most Windows programs, before you can carry out an action on part of a database, you must first select it. Selected data is highlighted as shown below.

Selecting Fields

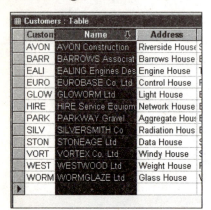

A field is a vertical column in a database table. To select it, move the mouse over the field name at the top of the column, and when the pointer changes to a ↓ shape, simply click to select the one field, or drag the pointer across several columns and release it to select those fields.

Selecting Records

A record, on the other hand, is a horizontal row in a database table. To select it, move the mouse into the area to the left of the record and when the pointer changes to a ⇒ shape, simply click to select the one record, or drag the pointer up or down across several rows and release it to select those records.

Selecting Cells

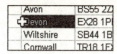

To select a cell, move the mouse over the left edge of the cell and the pointer will change to a ⇧ shape. Simply click this pointer to select the cell, or drag it across the required cells and release it to select more than one.

Selecting Data in a Cell

To select data in a cell, position the I pointer in the data, left-click and drag the pointer to highlight the required data, as shown here.

Zooming into a Cell

If you need to view or edit the contents of a cell that are not visible in a table because the column width is too narrow, you can open a zoom window on the cell. To do this, click the cell and press the <Shift+**F2**> key combination.

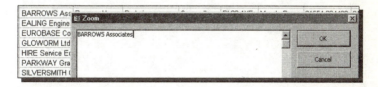

Once the Zoom dialogue box opens, you can view the whole content of the cell. You can edit the cell contents in this box as well, which makes life far easier as you can see what you are doing.

When you have finished with the cell, click the **OK** button to close the Zoom box. Any changes you made will be automatically saved for you.

Working with Data

Adding Records in a Table

 Whether you are in Table view or Form view, to add a record, click the New Record icon, shown here.

When in Table view, the cursor jumps to the first empty record in the table (the one with the asterisk in the box to the left of the first field). When in Form view, Access displays an empty form which can be used to add a new record.

Finding Records in a Table

 In Table or Form view, to find a record click the Find icon, use **Edit, Find**, or the <Ctrl+F> key combination. These all open the following Find and Replace dialogue box:

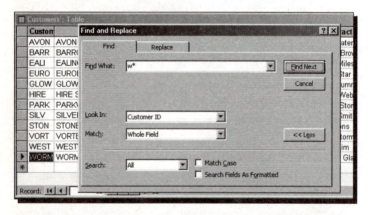

Note the field name in the **Look In** box, which is CustomerID, indicating that the cursor was in the CustomerID field before we actioned the Find command.

To find all the records starting with **w**, we typed **w*** in the **Find What** box. Pressing the **Find Next** button, highlights the first record with the CustomerID 'WEST', in our case.

Pressing the **Find Next** button again, highlights the next record that matches our selected criteria.

Clicking the Replace tab opens the very powerful tool for replacing one text string for another, in individual fields, or whole tables or forms.

Deleting Records from a Table

 To delete a record when in Table view, point to the box to the left of the record to highlight the entire record, then either right-click and select **Delete Record**, as shown below, click the Delete Record icon on the main toolbar, or press the <Del> key.

To delete a record when in Form view, first display the record you want to delete, then click the Delete Record icon on the main toolbar.

In both cases you will be given a warning and you will be asked to confirm your decision.

Manipulating Table Columns

Perhaps the easiest way to manipulate the columns of an Access table is to select the column, or columns, and use the menu that is opened by right-clicking the column, as shown here.

This gives a range of rapid options that are available. You can sort the column, or field, in ascending or descending order, **Copy** the column contents to the clipboard, and then **Paste** them to an empty column, either in the same table, or in another one.

Adjusting Column Widths

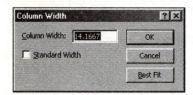

Selecting **Column Width** from the above menu opens the small box shown here, which gives you three options. You can type an exact width in the **Column Width** text box, select **Standard Width** to force the Access default width of about one 'screen inch', or click **Best Fit**. The last option sets the column width so that both the heading and all field values are visible. Not much use if you have long text items in your fields, but excellent for more simple columns.

On page 42 we saw that an easy, if imprecise, way to change the width of a column was to drag the ✛ shaped pointer in the column selector at the top of a column. There is also a quick way to select the 'Best Fit' width for a column, by double-clicking this ✛ pointer on the right border of the column selector.

Hiding Fields

To reduce the data displayed on the screen you may find it useful to hide one or more columns, by first selecting them and then using the **Hide Columns** command, from either the right-click shortcut menu, or the **Format** menu.

A hidden field is, of course, not deleted from the database, it is just made temporarily invisible. To unfreeze fields simply use the **Format**, **Unhide Columns** menu command.

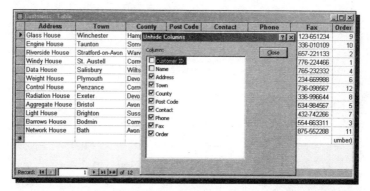

This opens the dialogue box shown above. In this example we have hidden two fields, to unhide them we would need to check their boxes in the **Column** list and click **Close**.

Freezing Fields

The **Freeze Columns** menu option, from either the right-click shortcut menu, or the **Format** menu, moves selected columns to the left of a table and always displays them.

You can only cancel this operation from the **Format** menu with the **Unfreeze All Columns** command.

This, however, leaves the previously frozen columns still moved to the left of the table. As long as you have not saved the table with its columns frozen, you can close the table (without saving it) and re-open it in its original state. If you have saved the table, to return it to its original format you will have to move the fields back to where they 'started'.

Moving a Field

To move a field from its current position to a new position in

a table, select the field you want to move, make sure it is not frozen, then click on the column selector so that the mouse pointer changes to that shown here, and drag the row to its new position.

Note that while you are dragging the field, a solid vertical bar shows where the field will be placed when the mouse button is released, as shown above.

Inserting, Renaming and Deleting Fields

To insert a field in a table, select and highlight the field to the

right of where you want to insert the new field, right-click in it and select **Insert Column**, as shown in our composite here. You could also use the **Insert, Column** main menu command.

Select your new column, which above is named Field 1, and then use the **Rename Column** menu command, type the new name and press <Enter>. It's as easy as that.

To delete a field from a table, first select it, and then use the **Delete Column** shortcut menu command. You will be asked for confirmation before the column is actually deleted.

Adding a Lookup Column

There are times with most databases when a particular field requires only one of a limited number of possible entries. A

Contact	Title	Phone
John Waters	Mr	01657-113355
Mandy Brown		01554-664422
Trevor Miles	Mr	01336-010107
Sarah Star	Mrs	01736-098765
Peter Summe	Miss	01432-746523
Nicole Webb	Ms	01875-558822
James Stone	Dr	01534-987654
Adam Smith		01336-997755
Mike Irons		01765-234567
Brian Storm		01776-223344

good example might be the title field for the details of a person. These could be Mr, Mrs, Miss, Ms, Dr, etc. In Access you can include this list in a Lookup Column, as we show here.

When a cell is opened in this field a down-arrow button appears which, when clicked, opens the list of possibilities for you to choose from. Anything that saves time and typing when adding data has to be good news!

To open the Wizard to add such a column, select the column to the right of where you want it to be, right-click in it, and select **Lookup Column** from the shortcut menu.

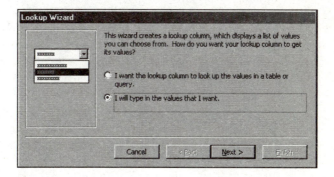

Opt to 'type in the values that I want' and click **Next** to go to the next Wizard box shown completed below.

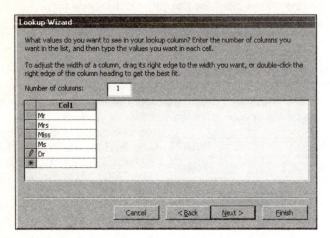

Make sure you select '1' as the **Number of columns** and then type the list entries one at a time. To move to the next cell press the <Tab> key. When you are happy with your list click the **Next** button and type in a suitable label for the field column. In our example 'Title' would be suitable, then click **Finish** to do just that.

Editing a Lookup List

If you need to make changes to a Lookup list in the future you can do it in the Design View of a database table.

In this view, click the field with the Lookup column and then select the **Lookup** tab, as shown on the next page. In the Row Source section of the Field Properties list you can see the values that will appear in the Lookup column.

You can edit this list as you wish, but make sure you keep its format intact. Items are included in inverted commas ("") and separated with semicolons (;).

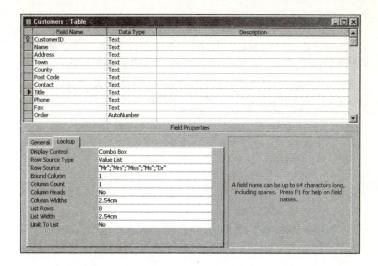

Printing a Table View

You can print a database table by clicking the Print icon, or by using the **File, Print** command to display the usual Windows Print dialogue box shown below. Alternatively, you can preview a database on screen with the **Print Preview** menu command, or toolbar icon.

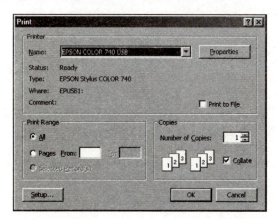

However, printing directly from here, produces a predefined print-out, the format of which you cannot control, apart from the margins and print orientation. To control these, select the **Page Setup** menu option shown on the previous page.

For a better method of producing a printed output, see the Report Design section in a later chapter.

5

Relational Database Design

In order to be able to discuss relational databases, we will add an Orders table to the database of the previous chapter. To do this go through the following steps.

- Open the **Adept 1** database, select **Tables** from the **Objects** list in the Database window and use the **New** button to add an Orders table to it.

- Select **Table Wizard** from the New Table box and select Orders from the displayed **Sample Tables** list. Next, select the five fields displayed below under **Fields in my new table** from the Sample Fields list, and press the **Next** button.

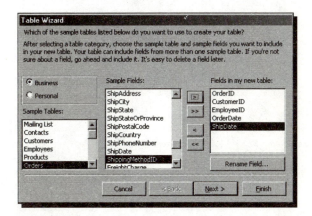

This displays the top dialogue box on the next page, in which you can, if you want, change the name of the table. We elected to accept the default name, but we clicked the **No, I'll set the primary key** radio button before pressing the **Next** key.

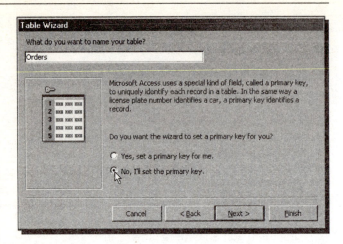

- In the next dialogue box you can select which field will hold data that is unique for each record. The key field must be unique in a table, and the OrderID field satisfies this requirement. This field is used by Access for fast searches.

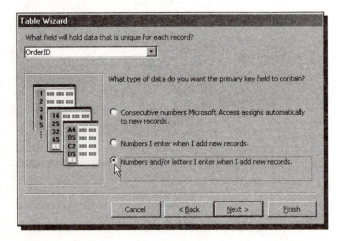

- Click the **Numbers and/or letters I enter when I add new records** radio button, before you press the **Next** button again.

On the next dialogue box you specify whether the new table is related to any other tables in the database. The default being 'not related'.

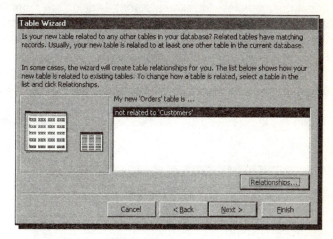

• Accept the default option, and press the **Next** button to reveal the final dialogue box.

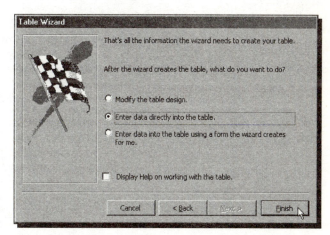

• Select the second option and press the **Finish** button, to let the Wizard create your table.

Although the two tables are actually related, we chose at this stage to tell the Wizard that they are not. This might appear to you as odd, but the Wizard makes certain assumptions about unique fields (for example, that ID fields are numbers), which is not what we want. We chose to remain in control of the design of our database and, therefore, we will define the relationship between the two tables later.

The Wizard displays the newly created table ready for you to enter your data. However, before doing so, use the Design Table facility, as discussed previously, to change the Data Types of the selected Field Names to those displayed below.

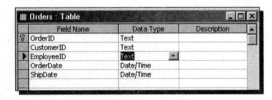

The information you need to enter in the Orders table is shown below.

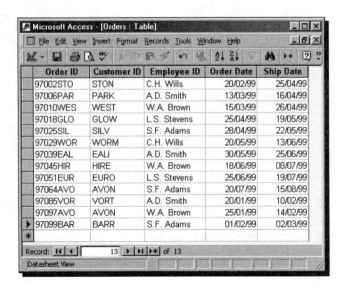

Relationships

Information held in two or more tables of a database is normally related in some way. In our case, the two tables, Customers and Orders, are related by the CustomerID field.

To build up relationships between tables, press the Relationships icon on the main Access Toolbar, shown here. This opens the following window in which the index field in each table is emboldened.

You can build relationships between tables by dragging a field name from one table into another. In our example above, we have dragged CustomerID from the Customers table (by pointing to it, pressing the left mouse button, and keeping the mouse button pressed, moving the pointer) to the required field in the other table, in this case CustomerID in the Orders table. Releasing the mouse button opens the dialogue box shown here.

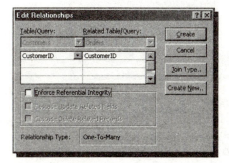

Pressing the **Join Type** button on this Edit Relationships dialogue box opened yet another box for our attention.

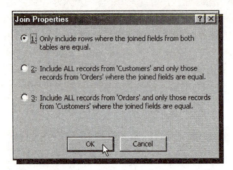

In this Join Properties dialogue box you can specify the type of join Access should create in new queries - more about this later. For the present, press the OK button on the Join Properties dialogue box, to close it, then check the **Enforce Referential Integrity** box in the Edit Relationships dialogue box, and press the **Create** button.

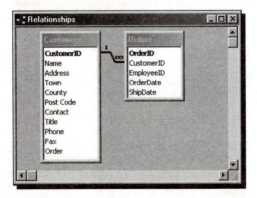

Access creates and graphically displays the chosen type of relationship in the Relationships window shown here. Note the relationship '1 customer to many (∞) orders' symbolism in the Relationships window. Before leaving the Relationships window Access will ask if you want to save your changes, which you probably do.

Because Access is a relational database, data can be used in queries from more than one table at a time. As we have seen, if the database contains tables with related data, the relationships can be defined easily.

Usually, the matching fields have the same name, as in our example of Customers and Orders tables. In the Customers table, the CustomerID field is the primary field and relates to the CustomerID field in the Orders table - there can be several orders in the Orders table from one customer in the Customers table.

The various types of relationships are as follows:

- Inherited - for attaching tables from another Access database. The original relationships of the attached database can be used in the current database.

- Referential - for enforcing relationships between records according to certain rules, when you add or delete records in related tables belonging to the same database. For example, you can only add records to a related table, if a matching record already exists in the primary table, and you cannot delete a record from the primary table if matching records exist in a related table.

Viewing and Editing Relationships

At any time you can view the current relationships between tables, by clicking the Relationships icon and opening the Relationships dialogue box.

To edit a relationship, double-click the left mouse button on the inclined line joining the two tables. If you have difficulty with this action, first point to the relationship line and click once to embolden it, then use the **Relationships**, **Edit Relationship** command. Either of these two actions will open the Edit Relationships dialogue box in which you can change the various options already discussed.

A given relationship can easily be removed altogether by first activating it (pointing and clicking to embolden it), then pressing the Clear Layout Toolbar button. A confirmation dialogue box will be displayed, as shown below.

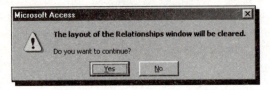

To delete a table, you must first detach it from other tables, then select it in the Database window and press the Delete button. Think before you do this!

Creating an Additional Table

As an exercise, create a third table using the Table Wizard and select Invoices from the displayed **Sample Tables** list. Next, select the five fields displayed below in Design View - the names and their data types have been changed as shown.

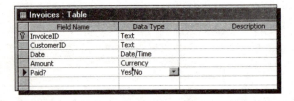

Next, enter the data given on the next page and build up appropriate relationships between the Invoices table, the Customers table and the Orders table, as also shown on the next page.

Invoice No	Customer ID	Date	Amount	Paid?
AD9701	VORT	25/04/99	£120.84	No
AD9702	AVON	16/04/99	£103.52	Yes
AD9703	BARR	26/04/99	£99.32	No
AD9704	STON	19/05/99	£55.98	No
AD9705	PARK	22/05/99	£180.22	No
AD9706	WEST	13/06/99	£68.52	No
AD9707	GLOW	25/06/99	£111.56	No
AD9708	SILV	08/07/99	£123.45	Yes
AD9709	WORM	19/07/99	£35.87	No
AD9710	EALI	15/08/99	£58.95	No
AD9711	HIRE	10/02/99	£290.00	No
AD9712	EURO	14/02/99	£150.00	No
AD9713	AVON	02/03/99	£135.00	No

The relationships between the three tables should be arranged as follows:

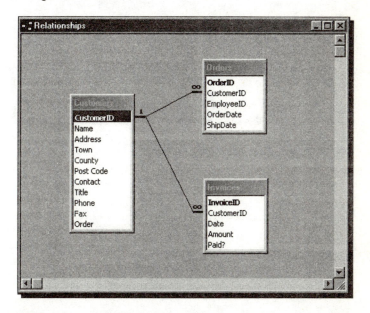

Once the relationships between tables have been established, you can create queries, forms, and reports to display information from several tables at once.

It is important that you should complete this exercise, as it consolidates what we have done so far and we will be using all three tables in what comes next. So go ahead and try it.

If you need more help coming to terms with database relationships there is a lot of detail in the Access Help facility, as shown below. A good place to start would be the section *About relationships in an Access database.*

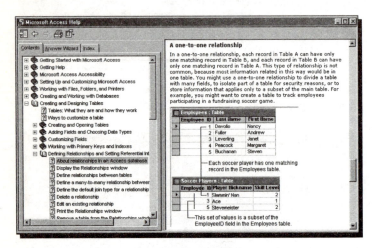

6

Creating a Query

In Access you create a query so that you can ask questions about the data in your database tables. For example, we could find out whether we have more than one order from the same customer in our Adept database.

To do this, start Access, load the **Adept 1** database, and in the Database window click the Queries button in the **Objects** column, followed by the **New** button which opens the New Query dialogue box shown below.

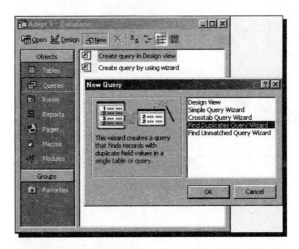

Selecting **Find Duplicates Query Wizard**, as shown here, and clicking **OK** opens the first of the Find Duplicates Query Wizard dialogue boxes which are all displayed in the series of screen-dumps on the next page.

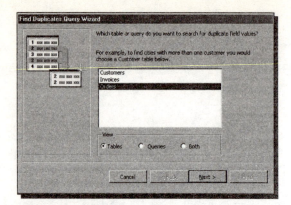

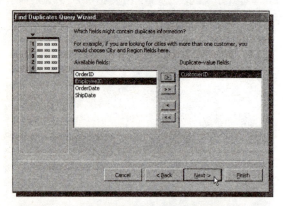

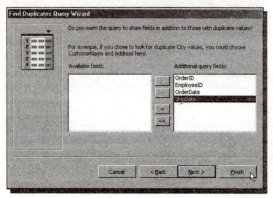

In the top box select the Orders table from the displayed database tables and press the **Next** button.

In the following dialogue box select **CustomerID** as the field you want to check for duplicate values, then press the 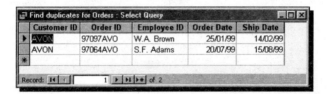 button, followed by the **Next** button.

Finally, select the additional fields you would like to see along with the duplicate values, by selecting those you want from the last dialogue box, either one at a time or, if you decide to select all of them, as shown here, by clicking the **>>** button. Clicking the **Finish** button then displays the Select Query window shown below.

Customer ID	Order ID	Employee ID	Order Date	Ship Date
AVON	97097AVO	W.A. Brown	25/01/99	14/02/99
AVON	97064AVO	S.F. Adams	20/07/99	15/08/99

Record: 1 of 2

If you examine the original Orders table, you will indeed find that it contains two orders from AVON. When you close this window, by clicking its ✕ close button, you will find the new entry 'Find duplicates for Orders' has been added to the Queries list in the Database window, as shown below.

Once a query has been set up in Access you can action it at any time by double-clicking its name in the database Window.

Types of Queries

The query we have created so far, is known as a *Select Query*, which is the most common type of query. However, with Access you can also create and use other types of queries, as follows:

- **Crosstab query** - used to present data with row and column headings, just like a spreadsheet. These can be used to summarise large amounts of data in a more readable form.

- **Action queries** - used to make changes to many records in one operation. They can consist of make-table, delete, update and append queries. For example, you might like to remove from a given table all records that meet certain criteria. Obviously, this type of query has to be treated with care!

- **Union query** - used to match fields from two or more tables.

- **Pass-through query** - used to pass commands to a SQL (pronounced 'sequal') database (see below).

- **Data-definition query** - used to create, change, or delete tables in an Access database using SQL statements.

- **Subquery** - consists of an SQL SELECT statement inside another select query or action query.

SQL stands for Structured Query Language, often used to query, update, and manage relational databases. Each query created by Access has an associated SQL statement that defines the action of that query. Thus, if you are familiar with SQL, you can use such statements to view and modify queries, or set form and report properties. However, these actions can be done more easily with the QBE (query-by-example) grid, to be discussed next. If you design union queries, pass-through queries, or data-definition queries, then you must use SQL statements, as these types of queries can not be designed with the QBE grid.

Finally, to create a sub-query, you use the QBE grid, but you enter an SQL SELECT statement for criteria, as we shall see in the next QBE grid example.

The Query Window

The Query window is a graphical query-by-example (QBE) tool. Because of Access' graphical features, you can use the mouse to select, drag, and manipulate objects in the query window to define how you would like to see your data.

An example of a ready made Query window can be seen by selecting the Find duplicates for Orders query and clicking the **Design** button on the Database window. This action opens the Select Query dialogue box shown below.

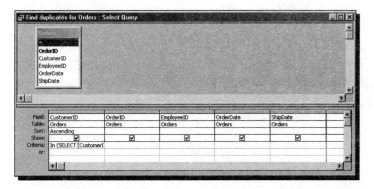

You can add a table to the top half of the Query window by simply dragging it from the Database window. To remove it again, simply right-click in it and select **Remove Table** from the shortcut menu. Similarly, you can add fields to the bottom half of the Query window (the QBE grid) by dragging fields from the tables on the top half of the Query window. In addition, the QBE grid is used to select the sort order of the data, or insert criteria, such as SQL statements.

To see the full SQL SELECT statement written by Access as the criteria selection when we first defined the query, use the **View, SQL View** command.

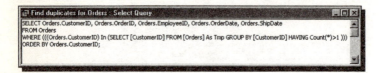

Note the part of the statement which states 'As Tmp GROUP'. Access collects the data you want as a temporary group, called a *dynaset*. This special set of data behaves like a table, but it is not a table; it is a dynamic view of the data from one or more tables, selected and sorted by the particular query.

Creating a New Query

Another way to create a new query is in the Design view. In the Database window, first click the Queries button in the **Objects** list and then double-click the option **Create query in Design view**. This opens both the Select Query and the Show Table dialogue boxes shown overleaf.

In our example, the Invoices and Customers tables were then added to the Select Query window, by selecting each in the Show Table box and clicking the **Add** button.

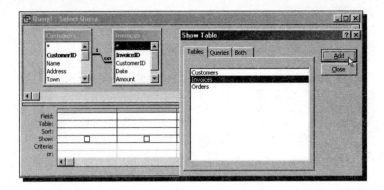

Adding Fields to a Query Window

Below we show a screen in which the Paid? and InvoiceID fields have been dragged from the Invoices table and added to the Query window. In addition, the Name and Contact fields have been dragged from the Customers table and placed on the Query window, while the Phone field from the Customers table is about to be added to the Query window.

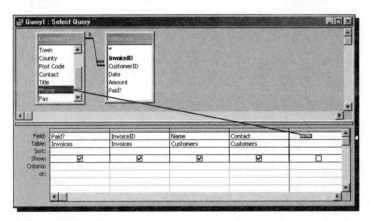

Having dragged these five fields, plus the Amount field, from the two tables onto the QBE grid, we have added the word 'No' as the criteria on the Paid? field and selected Ascending as the Sort for the InvoiceID field.

Note that the Invoices and Customers tables are joined by a line that connects the two CustomerID fields. The join line was created when we designed the tables and their relationships in the previous chapter. Even if you have not created these relationships, Access will join the tables in a query automatically when the tables are added to a query, provided each table has a field with the same name and a compatible data type and one of those fields is a primary key. A primary field is displayed in bold in the Query window.

If you have not created relationships between your tables yourself, or Access has not joined your tables automatically, you can still use related data in your query by joining the tables in the Query window.

 Clicking the Run icon on the Toolbar, shown here, instantly displays all the unpaid invoices with the details you have asked for, as follows:

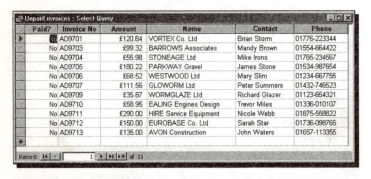

Paid?	Invoice No	Amount	Name	Contact	Phone
No	AD9701	£120.84	VORTEX Co. Ltd	Brian Storm	01776-223344
No	AD9703	£99.32	BARROWS Associates	Mandy Brown	01554-664422
No	AD9704	£55.98	STONEAGE Ltd	Mike Irons	01765-234567
No	AD9705	£180.22	PARKWAY Gravel	James Stone	01534-987654
No	AD9706	£68.52	WESTWOOD Ltd	Mary Slim	01234-667755
No	AD9707	£111.56	GLOWORM Ltd	Peter Summers	01432-746523
No	AD9709	£35.87	WORMGLAZE Ltd	Richard Glazer	01123-654321
No	AD9710	£58.95	EALING Engines Design	Trevor Miles	01336-010107
No	AD9711	£290.00	HIRE Service Equipment	Nicole Webb	01875-558822
No	AD9712	£150.00	EUROBASE Co. Ltd	Sarah Star	01736-098765
No	AD9713	£135.00	AVON Construction	John Waters	01657-113355

To save your newly created query, use the **File, Save As** command, and give it a name such as 'Unpaid invoices' in the Save As dialogue box. If you don't do this, you will be given the option to save the query when you close the Select Query results window above.

Once saved you can action this query whenever you like from the Database window, and get a current list of what unpaid invoices are outstanding at the time.

Types of Criteria

Access accepts the following expressions as criteria:

Arithmetic Operators		Comparison Operators		Logical Operators	
*	Multiply	<	Less than	And	And
/	Divide	<=	Less than or equal	Or	Inclusive or
+	Add	>	Greater than	Xor	Exclusive or
-	Subtract	>=	Greater than or equal	Not	Not equivalent
		=	Equal	Eqv	Equivalent
		<>	Not equal	Imp	Implication
Other operators					
Between	Between 50 And 150	All values between 50 and 150			
In	In("Bath","Bristol")	All records with Bath and Bristol			
Is	Is Null	All records with no value in that field			
Like	Like "Brian *"	All records with Brian something in field			
&	[Name]&" "&[Surname]	Concatenates strings			

Using Wildcard Characters in Criteria

In an example on page 44 we used the criteria W* to mean any company whose name starts with the letter W. The asterisk in this criteria is known as a wildcard character.

To search for a pattern, you can use the asterisk (*) and the question mark (?) as wildcard characters when specifying criteria in expressions. An asterisk stands for any number of characters, while a question mark stands for any single character in the same position as the question mark.

The following examples show the use of wildcard characters in various types of expressions:

Entered Expression	Meaning	Examples
a?	Any two-letter word beginning with A	am, an, as, at
???d	Any four-letter word ending with d	find, hand, land yard
Sm?th	Any five-letter word beginning with Sm and ending with th	Smith Smyth
fie*	Any word starting with the letters fie	field, fiend, fierce, fiery
*ght	Any word ending with ght	alight, eight, fight, light, might, sight
*/5/99	All dates in May '99	1/5/99
a	Any word with the letter a in it	Brian, Mary, star, yard

Combining Criteria

By specifying additional criteria in a Query window you can create powerful queries for viewing your data. In the examples below we have added extra criteria to our Unpaid Invoices query.

To follow these on your PC just open the Query in Design view from the Database window.

The AND Criteria with Different Fields: When you insert criteria in several fields, but in the same row, Access assumes that you are searching for records that meet all of the criteria. In the next example, the criteria should list the records with an Amount outstanding of between £50 and £150, and where the Contact name begins with 'M'. The second criteria can be entered as M*, and Access will convert this to Like "M*".

Field:	Paid?	InvoiceID	Amount	Name	Contact	
Table:	Invoices	Invoices	Invoices	Customers	Customers	
Sort:		Ascending				
Show:	☑	☑	☑	☑	☑	
Criteria:	No		Between 50 And 150		Like "M*"	
or:						

Unpaid invoices : Select Query

	Paid?	Invoice No	Amount	Name	Contact	Phone
▶	No	AD9703	£99.32	BARROWS Associates	Mandy Brown	01554-664422
	No	AD9704	£55.98	STONEAGE Ltd	Mike Irons	01765-234567
	No	AD9706	£68.52	WESTWOOD Ltd	Mary Slim	01234-667755

Record: ◄ ◄ | 1 | ► ►I ►* of 3

The OR Criteria with the Same Field: If you include multiple criteria in one field only, then Access assumes that you are searching for records that meet any one of the specified criteria. For example, the criteria <50 or >100 in the field Amount, shown below, list the required records, only if the No in the Paid? field is inserted in both rows.

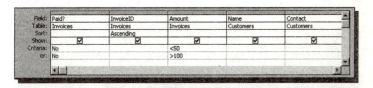

Unpaid invoices : Select Query

	Paid?	Invoice No	Amount	Name	Contact
▶	No	AD9701	£120.84	VORTEX Co. Ltd	Brian Storm
	No	AD9705	£180.22	PARKWAY Gravel	James Stone
	No	AD9707	£111.56	GLOWORM Ltd	Peter Summers
	No	AD9709	£35.87	WORMGLAZE Ltd	Richard Glazer
	No	AD9711	£290.00	HIRE Service Equipment	Nicole Webb
	No	AD9712	£150.00	EUROBASE Co. Ltd	Sarah Star
	No	AD9713	£135.00	AVON Construction	John Waters

Record: ◄ ◄ | 1 | ► ►I ►* of 7

The OR Criteria with Different Fields: If you include multiple criteria in different fields, but in different rows, then Access assumes that you are searching for records that meet either one or the other of the specified criteria. For example, the criteria Yes in the Paid? field and <50 in the Amount field, but in different rows, list the following records.

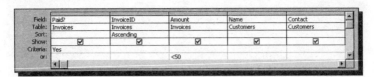

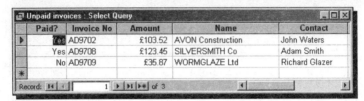

The AND and OR Criteria Together: The following choice of criteria will cause Access to retrieve either records that have Yes in the Paid? field and the company's name starts with the letter A, or records with an invoice amount of less than £50.

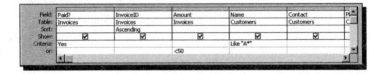

The retrieved records from such a query are shown below.

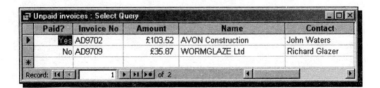

Creating Calculated Fields

Let's assume that we want to increase the amounts payable on all invoices overdue by more than 30 days from today by 0.5%, as a penalty for not settling on time. We can achieve this by creating a calculated field in our database.

To create a calculated field, open **Adept 1**, click the Query button in the Database window, select the Unpaid invoices query, and click the **Design** button on the Toolbar. Next, insert a field after the Amount field by highlighting the column after it and using the **Insert**, **Columns** command. Now type in the Field row of the newly inserted empty column, the following information:

```
New Amount:[Amount]*1.005
```

where *New Amount:* is our chosen name for the calculated field - the colon is essential. If you do not supply a name for the calculated field, Access uses the default name *Expr1:*, which you can rename later. The square brackets enclosing the word Amount in the above expression indicate a field name.

 Next, click the Properties button, shown here, or use the **View**, **Properties** command, to set the Format property to Currency.

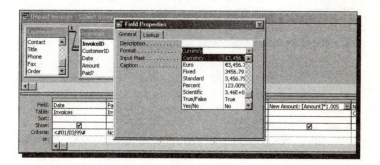

Finally, add the Date field from the Invoices table to our query and type the expression <#01/03/99# in its Criteria field - the hash marks and leading zeros are supplied by Access if you do not type them yourself.

Clicking either of the Datasheet View, or Run, buttons on the Toolbar, displays the following results:

We suggest you save this query under the name Penalty invoices.

Using Functions in Criteria

There are several functions that you can use in a calculated field of an Access query which can either be applied to extract information from text or date fields, or be used to calculate totals of entries.

Finding Part of a Text Field

Let us assume that you want to find information that is part of a text field, like the area code (first 5 numbers) in the Phone field of our Customers table. To help you search a table for only part of a text field, Access provides three string functions. The syntax of these functions is as follows:

```
Left(stringexpr,n)
Right(stringexpr,n)
Mid(stringexpr,start,n)
```

The *stringexpr* argument can be either a field name or a text expression, while *n* is the number of characters you are searching for, and *start* is the position of the first character you want to start from.

Thus, to extract the area code of the text field Phone in our Customers table, open the Unpaid Invoices query, click the Design View button on the toolbar, and type in the Field row of an empty field, either

```
Area Codes:Left([Phone],5)
```
or
```
Area Codes:Mid([Phone],1,5)
```

Note that to distinguish between the name of a field and a text expression, the name of the field is enclosed in square brackets.

Next, click the Datasheet View button on the toolbar. The result of such a query is displayed below.

Paid?	Invoice No	Amount	Name	Contact	Phone	Area Codes
No	AD9701	£120.84	VORTEX Co. Ltd	Brian Storm	01776-223344	01776
No	AD9703	£99.32	BARROWS Associates	Mandy Brown	01554-664422	01554
No	AD9704	£55.98	STONEAGE Ltd	Mike Irons	01765-234567	01765
No	AD9705	£180.22	PARKWAY Gravel	James Stone	01534-987654	01534
No	AD9706	£68.52	WESTWOOD Ltd	Mary Slim	01234-667755	01234
No	AD9707	£111.56	GLOWORM Ltd	Peter Summers	01432-746523	01432
No	AD9709	£35.87	WORMGLAZE Ltd	Richard Glazer	01123-654321	01123
No	AD9710	£58.95	EALING Engines Design	Trevor Miles	01336-010107	01336
No	AD9711	£290.00	HIRE Service Equipment	Nicole Webb	01875-558822	01875
No	AD9712	£150.00	EUROBASE Co. Ltd	Sarah Star	01736-098765	01736
No	AD9713	£135.00	AVON Construction	John Waters	01657-113355	01657

Record: 14 4 | 12 | ▶ ▶I ▶* of 12

Finding Part of a Date Field

To extract part of a date field, such as the month in which unpaid invoices were issued, type

```
Month:DatePart("m",[Date])
```

in the Field row of an empty field.

To extract the year in which unpaid invoices were issued, type

```
Year:DatePart("yyyy",[Date])
```

in the Field row of an empty field. This function returns the year in four digits, such as 1999.

The result of such a query is shown below.

Calculating Totals in Queries

It is possible that you might want to know the total value of outstanding invoices grouped by month. Access allows you to perform calculations on groups of records using *totals* queries, also known as *aggregate* queries.

Function	Used to Find
Avg	The average of values in a field
Count	The number of values in a field
First	The field value from the first record in a table or query
Last	The field value from the last record in a table or query
Max	The highest value in a field
Min	The lowest value in a field
StDev	The standard deviation of values in a field
Sum	The total of values in a field
Var	The variance of values in a field

The table on the previous page lists the functions that can be used in queries to display totals. These functions are entered in the Totals row of a query which can be displayed by clicking the Totals button, shown here, while in Design View.

Below we show the one-table query to find the total value of unpaid invoices grouped by month.

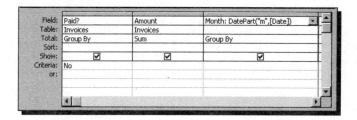

The retrieved records from such a query are shown below. We have named this query 'Monthly invoices'.

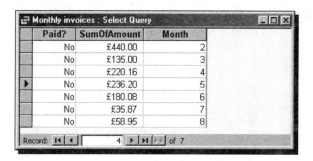

Paid?	SumOfAmount	Month
No	£440.00	2
No	£135.00	3
No	£220.16	4
No	£236.20	5
No	£180.08	6
No	£35.87	7
No	£58.95	8

Record: |◄| ◄| 4 |►|►I|►*| of 7

7

More Advanced Queries

We have seen in the last chapter how to create a query with fields taken from two tables. The query in question was Unpaid invoices, shown below in Design view.

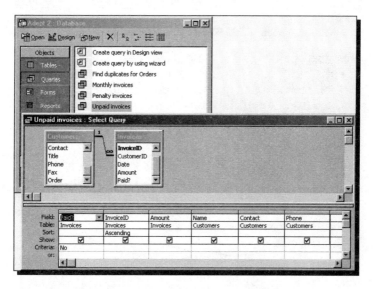

To make it easier for us to know which field in the above query comes from which table, Access displays the name of the table by default. This option is controlled from the **View, Table Names** command when in Design view. When this menu option is ticked, Access adds the Table row in the QBE grid.

 Now, suppose we would like to add the Orders table so that we can see the OrdersID field in extracted records of our query. To do this, click the Show Table button, shown here, which opens the Show

Table dialogue box. Select Orders and click the **Add** button, then drag the OrdersID field onto the QBE grid, as shown below.

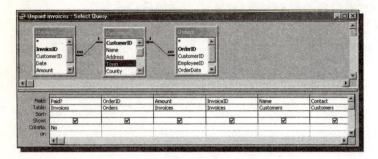

From this point on, we found it convenient to make a copy of **Adept 1.mdb** database and name it **Adept 2.mdb**. We did this for management purposes only. You, of course, can continue using **Adept 1.mdb**.

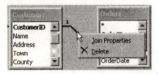

To find out what type of join exists between two tables, click the join line to highlight it, as shown here, then right-click and select **Join Properties** from the shortcut menu. This will open the following dialogue box:

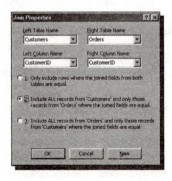

What we really need here is option 2. Select it so that the Query will extract the correct records.

Types of Joins

Microsoft Access supports the following types of joins:

Join Types	Effect
Equi-joins or Inner joins	A join in which records from two tables are combined and added to a dynaset only when there are equal values in the joined fields. For example, you can find records that show orders placed by each customer, with the dynaset containing only records for customers who have placed orders.
Outer joins	A join in which all the records from one table are added to the dynaset, and only those records from the other table for which values in the joined fields are equal. For example, you can find records that show all customers together with any orders they have placed.
Self-joins	A join in which records from one table are combined with other records from the same table when there are matching values in the joined fields. A self-join can be an equi-join or an outer join.

For an inner join, select option 1 from the Join Properties dialogue box. For an outer join, select option 2 or 3, depending on which records you want to include.

For example, choosing option 2 (also called a *left outer join*), displays all the required records from the Customers table and only those records from Orders where the joined fields are equal. Option 3 (also called a *right outer join*), on the other hand, attempts to display all records in Orders and only those records from Customers where the joined fields are equal, resulting in some confusion in our particular example.

Creating a Parameter Query

A *Parameter Query* is a variation of the *Select Query* - the type we have been using so far. A Parameter Query is used when you frequently run the same query, but need to change the criteria each time you run it. Instead of having to make changes to the QBE grid, the design of a Parameter Query forces Access to prompt you for criteria. This type of query is particularly useful when used as a filter with forms.

To design a Parameter Query, design a **New** query in the normal way (do not use the Query Wizards), or change an existing Select Query. We have chosen the latter route and selected to change the Penalty invoices query. In Design view, this now looks as follows:

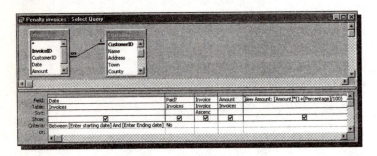

Note the two changes made to the above query. In the Date field we have entered two prompts (in square brackets) in the Criteria row, namely

```
[Enter starting date]
[Enter ending date]
```

and in the calculated field we have replaced the *1.005 by

```
*(1+[Percentage]/100)
```

When working with expressions like these, that are longer than the visible cell space available, it is often easier to use the Zoom window opened into the cell with the <Shift+**F2**> key strokes.

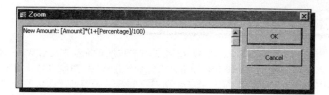

When this query is run, Access asks for input values in three successive Enter Parameter Value boxes, as shown below.

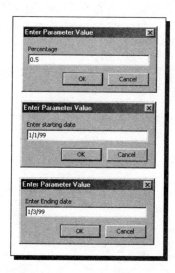

Providing the appropriate input information, displays the result of the search, as follows:

We have saved this query under the name 'Penalty invoices with parameters'.

Creating a Crosstab Query

You create a *Crosstab Query* to display totals in a compact, spreadsheet format. A Crosstab query can present a large amount of summary data in a more readable form. The layout of the extracted data from such a query is ideal as the basis for a report.

For example, suppose we wanted to examine which of our employees was responsible for our customers' orders in each month. The information is contained in the Orders table of our database as follows:

From the way this information is presented it is very difficult to work out who was responsible for which order in a given month. However, a Crosstab query that lists the names of the employees in rows and each month as a column heading, would be an ideal way to present this type of information.

To create a Crosstab query, open the **Adept 2** database and click first the Queries button, then the **New** button in the Database window. Next, select the **Crosstab Query Wizard** option from the list on the New Query dialogue box, as shown on the next page.

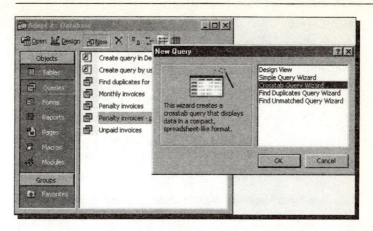

Pressing the **OK** button, opens the first Crosstab Query Wizard dialogue box on the screen. Select Orders from the displayed list of tables and press the **Next** button.

From the next dialogue box, select a maximum of three fields from the displayed list, which will become the row headings of the crosstab form. Choose OrderID, CustomerID, and EmployeeID, in that order, as shown below. The order you select these fields is important as Access will list the results of the query in alphabetical order of the first selected field.

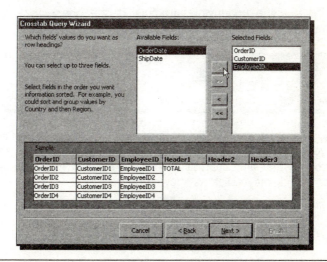

Having selected the three fields, click the **Next** button, and choose OrderDate as the field whose value you want as the column headings. Press **Next**, select Month as the time interval by which you want to group your columns and press **Next**. On the following dialogue box choose Count from the Functions list and press **Next**. Finally, accept the default name for the query, and press **Finish**.

The results of this Crosstab query are shown below with column widths set to Best Fit so that you can see the whole year at a glance.

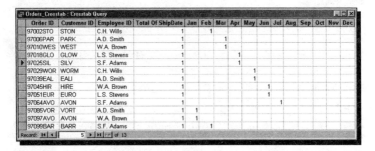

As you can see from the above screen, the required information is tabulated and is extremely easy to read. However, the displayed recordset is not updatable.

To see the underlying structure of the query, click the Design View button to display the QBE grid, as follows:

If you want to use a field for grouping, sorting, or setting criteria, but to exclude the field from the recordset, click the arrow in that field's Crosstab cell, and select **(not shown)** from the displayed list, as shown above.

Creating Queries for Updating Records

When a query is based on either a single table or on two tables with a one-to-one relationship, all the fields in the query are updatable.

Queries which include more than one table, when some of the tables have a one-to-many relationship, are more difficult to design so that they are updatable. Usually, such a query could be designed to be updatable, which is also true of a query that includes an attached table, unless the attached table is a SQL database table with no unique index.

The easiest way of finding out whether you can update records, is to design the query, run it and try to change values in its various fields and also add data. If you can not change values in a field or add data, then you will be warned with an appropriate message on the Status bar.

All other types of queries, such as a Crosstab query, a query with totals, a query with Unique Values property set to Yes, a Union Query, a Pass-through query, a calculated or read-only field, can not be used to update data.

For example, if you try to change the second name under Employee ID from Smith to Smyth, you get the message "This Recordset is not updatable" on the Status bar at the bottom of the screen, as shown below.

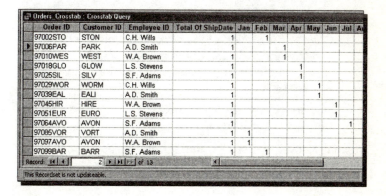

Order ID	Customer ID	Employee ID	Total Of ShipDate	Jan	Feb	Mar	Apr	May	Jun	Jul	Au
97002STO	STON	C.H. Wills	1		1						
97006PAR	PARK	A.D. Smith	1			1					
97010WES	WEST	W.A. Brown	1				1				
97018GLO	GLOW	L.S. Stevens	1					1			
97025SIL	SILV	S.F. Adams	1					1			
97029WOR	WORM	C.H. Wills	1						1		
97039EAL	EALI	A.D. Smith	1						1		
97045HIR	HIRE	W.A. Brown	1							1	
97051EUR	EURO	L.S. Stevens	1							1	
97064AVO	AVON	S.F. Adams	1								1
97085VOR	VORT	A.D. Smith	1	1							
97097AVO	AVON	W.A. Brown	1	1							
97099BAR	BARR	S.F. Adams	1		1						

Record: ⏮ ◀ 2 ▶ ⏭ of 13

This Recordset is not updateable.

Creating Action Queries

You can create *Action Queries* in the same way as Select Queries. Action Queries are used to make bulk changes to data rather than simply displaying data. For this reason, Action Queries can be dangerous for the novice, simply because they change your database.

There are four different types of Action Queries, with the following functions:

Type of Query	Function
Append query	Adds records from one or more tables to another table or tables.
Delete query	Deletes records from a table or tables.
Make-table query	Creates a new table from all or part of another table or tables.
Update query	Changes the data in a group of records

In a previous version of Access, you could quickly create an Action query which moved old orders to an Old Orders Archive table, by using the Archive Query Wizard. If you want to design such a query from scratch, then we suggest you go through the following steps:

- Use a Make-table query to copy selected records from an existing table into a new table, named, say, Old Orders Archive.

- Change the design of the Make-table query so that on subsequent execution of the query it Appends selected records from your original table to the Old Orders Archive table.

- Use the Delete query to delete the archived records from the original table.

In what follows, we will go through the steps necessary to create an Old Orders Archive query.

Open the database **Adept 2** and first click the Queries button in the Database window, then double-click on the Create query in design view option.

In the Show Table dialogue box that opens next, select Orders, as shown here, then press the **Add** button, followed by the **Close** button. This adds the Orders table to the Select Query window which also contains the QBE grid, so that you can design an appropriate query.

Drag all the fields from the Orders table onto the QBE grid, and add in the OrderDate field the criteria <=4/4/99, as shown below.

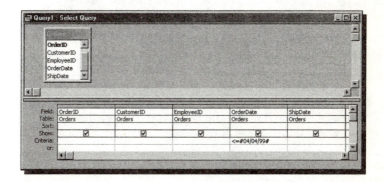

Click the arrow next to the Query Type button on the Toolbar, shown here, which displays the available query types. Select the **Make-Table Query** option which causes the Make Table dialogue box to appear on the screen.

Finally, type the name of the new table, say, Old Orders Archive, and press **OK**.

Pressing the Run Toolbar button causes a warning box to be displayed. In our example, we are told that six records are about to be pasted onto our new table.

Pressing **Yes**, copies the selected records from the Orders table to the newly created Old Orders Archive table.

Next, action the **Query**, **Append Query** menu command. The Append dialogue box is displayed with the Old Orders Archive name appearing as default. Press **OK** and close the Append Query window. When you click the 'X' button to close the Append Query window, you will be asked whether you would like your design to be saved. Select **Yes**, and in the displayed Save As dialogue box, type the new name for the query. We chose to call it Append to Old Orders Archive.

As an exercise, you could go through the steps of designing another Make Table query, but select the Delete option of the Query Type menu.

The next time you look at the Database window you should see that Access has placed two new queries in the Query list, as shown below. These have an exclamation point attached to their icon so that you don't run them inadvertently.

In all, there are four Action queries available in Access. Below we list these, together with their function.

1 The Make-Table query; used to create a table by retrieving the records that meet certain criteria and using them to create a new table.

2 The Append query; used to append (add) records from one table to another existing table.

3 The Update query; used to change data in existing tables, such as the cost per hour charged to your customers.

4 The Delete query; used to delete (remove) records that meet certain pre-defined criteria from a table.

Help on Queries

As we are sure you have found by now, the Help section of Access is essential reading when you are tackling a new section. We strongly recommend that you work your way through the section on Working with Queries, shown here.

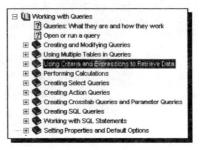

Below is a typical example of the depth of detail in some of the Help screens.

Examples of expressions that calculate or manipulate dates, and then use the result as criteria

Field	Expression	Description
RequiredDate	Between Date( ) And DateAdd ("m", 3, Date( ))	Uses the **Between...And** operator and the **DateAdd** and **Date** functions to display orders required between today's date and three months from today's date.
OrderDate	< Date( )- 30	Uses the **Date** function to display orders more than 30 days old.
OrderDate	Year([OrderDate])=1996	Uses the **Year** function to display orders with order dates in 1996.
OrderDate	DatePart("q", [OrderDate])=4	Uses the **DatePart** function to display orders for the fourth calendar quarter.
OrderDate	DateSerial(Year ([OrderDate]), Month([OrderDate])+1, 1)-1	Uses the **DateSerial**, Year, and **Month** functions to display orders for the last day of each month.
OrderDate	Year([OrderDate])= Year(Now()) And Month ([OrderDate])= Month(Now())	Uses the **Year** and **Month** functions and the **And** operator to display orders for the current year and month.

8

Using Forms

We saw towards the end of Chapter 4 how easy it was to create a single column form to view our Customers table. To see this again, open **Adept 1** and in the Database window click the Form button, then double-click on Customers, which should display the following:

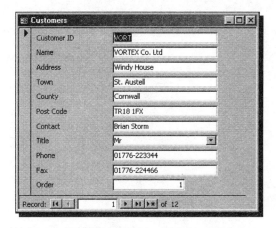

You can use forms to find, edit, and add data in a convenient manner - many people find them easier to work with than tables. Access provides you with an easy way of designing various types of forms, some of which are discussed here. Forms look good on screen, but do not produce very good output on paper, whereas reports, covered in the next chapter, are designed to look good on paper, but do not necessarily look good on screen.

Using the Form Wizard

Using the Form Wizard, you can easily display data from either a table or a query in Form view.

Open the **Adept 2** database, and in the Database window click the Forms button, then the **New** button which opens the New Form dialogue box in which you must choose either a table or a query on which to base the new form. In the screen dump below, we chose Form Wizard and the Customers table, before we clicked the **OK** button.

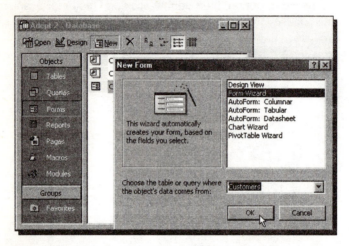

Creating a Form with a Subform

To help us enter new invoice data into our **Adept 2** database we will build a new form which holds the fields from the Customers table, but has a subform holding the Invoices table. So when the main form shows all the details of a particular customer, the subform will be visible with all the invoice information for that customer.

Before doing this you must make sure that your table relationships have been set up correctly. In our example, as long as you have followed our instructions, there should not be too many problems!

In the first wizard dialogue box, shown below, the table Customers should already be selected from the list. The two tables we are going to use have a one-to-many relationship, and Customers is the "one" side of this one-to-many relationship. In other words, every customer can have many invoices raised, but each invoice will only be relevant to one customer.

Double-click all the fields except Order in the **Available Fields** list to select them.

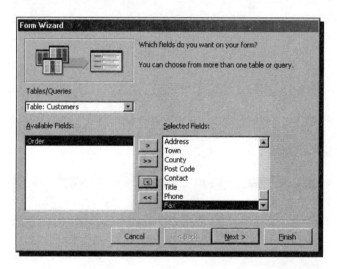

In the **same** wizard dialogue box, select the Invoices table from the **Tables/Queries** list and double-click all the fields except CustomerID, then click the **Next** button.

As long as you have set up the relationships correctly before starting the procedure, the wizard asks which table or query you want to view by. In our case to create the Customers form, click **by Customers**. In the same dialogue box, select the **Form with subform(s)** option, as shown on the next page and click the **Next** button.

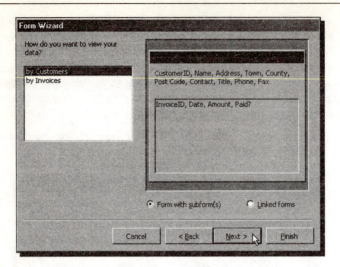

Select **Datasheet** layout and Standard style in the next two
wizard dialogue boxes, and name the **Form** Customer
Invoice Details as shown below.

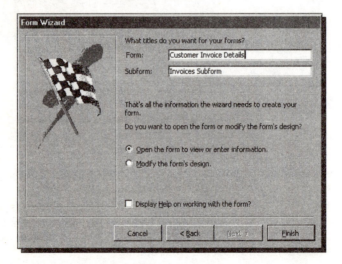

When you click **Finish**, Access creates two forms, one for
the main form and subform control, and one for the subform,
and opens the new form on the facing page.

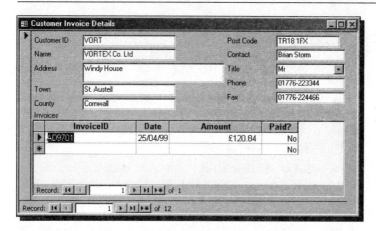

It's as easy as that with Access 2000. The form produced almost automatically is not yet perfect, but for most people would be adequate. We will customise it a little later on.

The other Form Wizards available are:

Type of Form	Function
AutoForm: Columnar	Creates a columnar form with all the field labels appearing in the first column and the data in the second. The form displays one record at a time.
AutoForm: Tabular	Tabulates a screen full of records in tabular form with the field labels appearing at the head of each column.
AutoForm: Datasheet	Similar to the Tabular form, but in worksheet display format.
Chart Wizard	Displays data graphically.
PivotTable Wizard	Creates a form with an Excel PivotTable - an interactive table that can summarise a large number of data using the format and calculation methods specified by the user.

Creating a Chart Form

As another example of using the Form Wizard we will step through the process of building a chart form to graphically show some of our data.

Open the **Adept 2** database, and in the Database window click the Forms button, then the **New** button, select Chart Wizard and the Invoices table, before clicking the **OK** button on the New Form dialogue box.

The Wizard will display a number of dialogue boxes. As before, after making appropriate selections, click the **Next** button to progress through the automatic design of the new form. To continue with our example, the Wizard displays the following dialogue box in which you are asked to specify the fields that contain the data you want to chart. We chose InvoiceID and Amount.

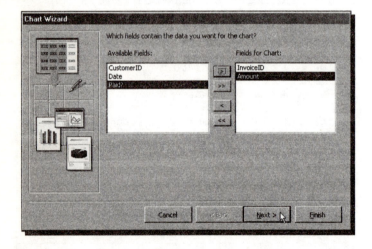

This opens another dialogue box in which you are asked what type of chart you would like. We chose Bar Chart, the first one on the second row before pressing **Next**, as shown at the top on the next page.

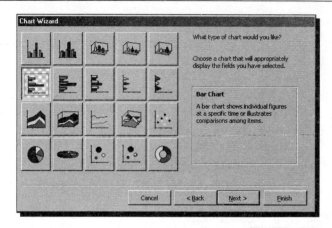

In the following dialogue box, double-click the x-axis button (the one with the caption 'SumOfAmount') and select 'None' from the list in the displayed Summarize dialogue box, shown below, and press **OK**.

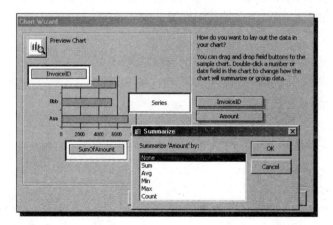

The Wizard then asks you what title to give to this form - we chose 'Invoice Amounts'.

Pressing the **Finish** button, allows the Wizard to display the final result, shown on the next page. It is as easy as that to get a graphical view of the amounts involved in each of your invoices. We named the form 'Invoice Chart'.

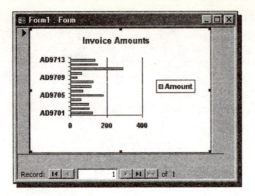

Customising a Form

You can customise a form by changing the appearance of text, data, and any other attributes. Below we show a slightly modified version of the Customer Invoice Details form in Design view. It is in this view that you make any changes to the design.

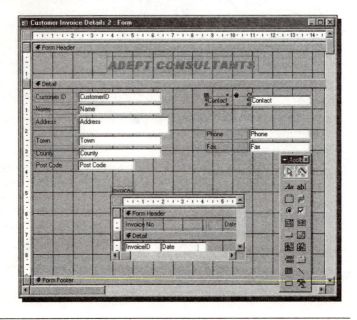

As you can see, a form in Design view is made up of boxes, or controls, attached to a grid. Clicking at the Contact box, for example, causes markers to appear around it as shown below. When the mouse pointer is then placed within either the label box or data box, it changes to a hand which indicates that you can drag the box to a new position. This method moves both label and data boxes together.

If you look more closely at the markers around the label and data boxes, you will see that they are of different size, as shown above.

The larger ones are 'move' handles, while the smaller ones are 'size' handles. In the above example you can use the 'move' handles of either the label or the data box to move one independently of the other.

Boxes on a form can be made larger or smaller by simply pointing to the sizing handles and dragging them in the appropriate direction.

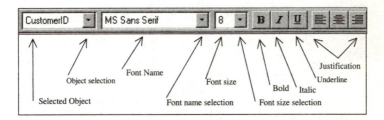

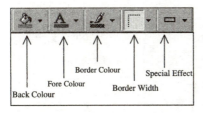

You can further customise a form using the various new buttons that appear on the Tool bar when in Design view, shown here in two tiers.

To use most of these buttons, you simply click the control (in Design view) that contains the feature you want to change and then click the button and make any selections you want.

Do try and experiment with moving and sizing label and data boxes and also increasing their font size. If you don't like the result, simply don't save it. Skills gained here will be used in the Report design section later on.

The Toolbox

The Toolbox can be used either to design a Form or Report from scratch (a task beyond the scope of this book), or to add controls to them, such as a Combo (drop-down) box. The function of each tool on the Toolbox is listed below and described on the following pages.

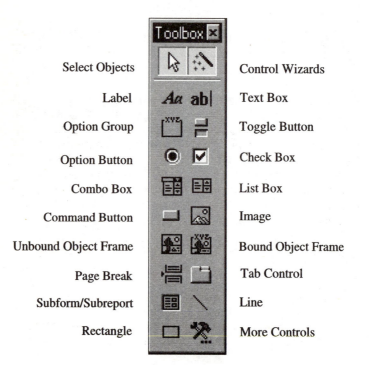

Select Objects	Control Wizards
Label	Text Box
Option Group	Toggle Button
Option Button	Check Box
Combo Box	List Box
Command Button	Image
Unbound Object Frame	Bound Object Frame
Page Break	Tab Control
Subform/Subreport	Line
Rectangle	More Controls

Aa Label

You use labels on a form, report, or data access page to display text such as titles or captions. Labels do not display values from fields, are always unbound (see below) and they stay the same between records.

When you create a label by using the Label tool, the label stands on its own and is not attached to any other control. When you create say a text box, it is automatically given an attached label that displays a caption for that text box. This label appears as a column heading in the Datasheet view of a form, whereas stand-alone labels don't appear in Datasheet view.

abl Text Box

Text boxes are used to display data from a record on a form, report, or a data access page. They are then said to be bound as they are directly linked to the field data.

Text boxes can also be unbound, or not linked to field data, say to display the results of a calculation or to accept input.

Toggle Button

A toggle button on a form is used to change the state of a field, for example to display a Yes/No, True/False, or On/Off value from an underlying record source. When you click a toggle button that is, say, bound to a Yes/No field in a database, the value in the underlying table displays according to the field's Yes/No property. You can use pictures on toggle buttons, with one picture representing one state of the field, and another when it is 'switched off'.

Toggle buttons are most used in option groups with other buttons.

Option Group

In a form or report, an option group consists of a group frame with a set of check boxes, option buttons, or toggle buttons. It is used to display a limited set of alternatives where only one can be selected at a time. An option group makes selecting a value easy because you can just click the value that you want.

◉ Option Button

You can use option buttons in three main ways:

- as a stand-alone control to display a Yes/No value from an underlying record source,

- in an option group to display values to choose from,

- in a custom dialogue box to accept user input.

With the first two uses the option buttons would be bound, and in the last unbound.

☑ Check Box

You can use a check box on a form, report, or data access page as a stand-alone control to display a Yes/No value from an underlying table, query, or SQL statement. If the box contains a check mark, the value is Yes; if it doesn't, the value is No.

▦ List Box

It is often quicker and easier to select a value from a list than to remember it and then type it into a form field. A list box gives this facility, and providing a fixed list of choices also helps prevent simple typing errors. In a form, a list box can have one or more columns. If a multiple-column list box is bound, Access stores the values from one of the columns.

▦ Combo Box

A combo box is like a text box and a list box combined. When you enter text or select a value in a bound combo box the entered or selected value is inserted into the field that the combo box is bound to.

On a form, you can use a combo box instead of a list box; it takes up less room, and you can type new values in it, as well as select values from a list.

Command Button

You use a command button on a form or data access page to start a macro to implement an action or a set of actions. The macro, or event procedure, must be attached to the button's OnClick property. You can create over thirty different types of command buttons with the Command Button Wizard.

Image

The image control is used to add unbound images, or pictures, to a form, as long as you will not need to edit them in the future. The images are stored in the database itself, which makes them very fast to load.

Unbound Object Frame

Unbound object frames can be used to add unbound images (or other objects like spreadsheet tables) to a frame or report when you may want to be able to edit them directly from the form or report. Double-clicking the image will then open the application that was used to create it so that you can edit it in-situ. The image is slower to load than with Image controls though.

Bound Object Frame

These are similar to the above but are used to display bound OLE objects (images or spreadsheet tables for example) that are actually stored in a table in the database. Double-clicking the object will then open the application that was used to create it so that you can edit it in-situ.

Tab Control

This can be used to present several pages of information as a single set on a form. Each page is given a headed tab and it is accessed by clicking on this tab.

▤ Page Break

The Page Break tool lets you design multiple screen (or page) forms. Remember to place page breaks above, or below, other controls to avoid splitting their data.

▦ Subform / Subreport

A subform is a form within a form and a subreport is a report within a report, the primary form or report being the main one, and the other the 'sub' one. These are especially effective when you want to show data from tables or queries with a one-to-many relationship, as we have seen in our example a few pages back.

╲ Line

Draws a line on a form, report, or data access page. Click anywhere on the form, report, or data access page to create a default-sized line. You can then click and drag it to create a line the size you want.

To make small adjustments to the length or angle of a line, select it, hold down the <Shift> key, and press one of the arrow keys. To make small adjustments in the placement of a line, hold down the <Ctrl> key and press one of the arrow keys. To change the thickness of a line, click the line, and click the arrow next to the Line/Border Width button on the toolbar and then click the line thickness you want. To change the line style to dots, dashes, etc., right-click the line, select **Properties** from the shortcut menu to open the Property sheet, and then click a border style in the BorderStyle property box, as shown here.

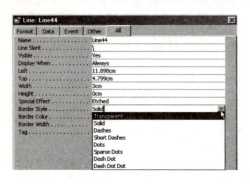

☐ Rectangle

Draws an 'empty' rectangle on a form, report, or data access page. You can change the size, colour and line thickness, etc., by editing the rectangle properties.

🛠 More Controls

On our PC this button opens a list of several hundred other control types to use. Most of these require extra software to be installed, but it is well worth experimenting here. The Calendar Control 9.0, for example worked with us, as shown below.

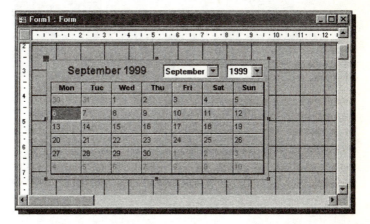

A calendar to be placed on any form in your database will surely have its uses, but you will have to experiment to find them.

We have played around with our Customer Invoice Details form in Design view, as can be seen at the top of the next page. You should not have too much trouble now with most of the changes. The title is formatted text inside a new Label control and several of the Text Boxes have been re-sized and moved, or even deleted! If you are interested, the vertical bar at the left of the form was removed by setting the 'Record Select' Form Property to No.

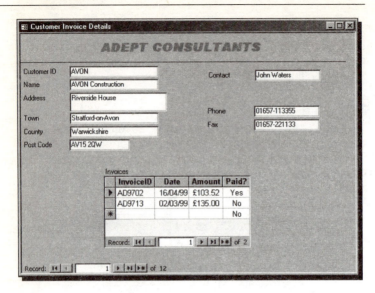

Adding a Combo Box

As an example of using the Toolbox in a form, we will step through the procedure of replacing the CustomerID text box field with a combo box, so that we can select from a drop-down menu when using this field. We will do this in a new form based on the Invoices table of the **Adept 2** database. You should have no trouble by now creating this form (as shown below) with the Form Wizard. Include all the table fields in it, and give it the name Add Invoices.

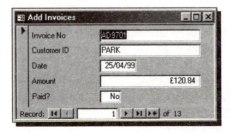

With this new Add Invoices form open in Design view, click the CustomerID field, and delete both its Label and Data boxes by clicking each individually and pressing the <Del> key.

 Click the Combo Box control on the Toolbox, and point and click at the area where the CustomerID field used to be on the form. In the subsequent dialogue boxes, select options which will cause the Combo Box to look up the values from the Customers table, and from the CustomerID field and store a selected value in the CustomerID field. Specify that the Combo Box should have the label Customer ID.

Move and size both the Label and Data boxes of the Combo box into the positions shown below.

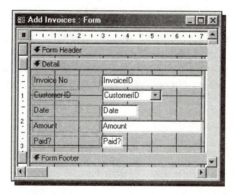

 Click the Form View button on the Toolbar, followed by the New Record button shown here. The entry form should now look like ours below:

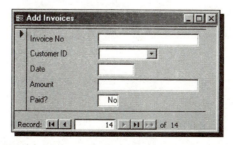

From now on, whenever you want to add a new invoice to the Invoices table, you can open this new form, then click the

New Record button on either the Toolbar or the form itself to display an empty form. Next, click the down arrow in the Customer ID field to display the drop-down menu shown here. Select one of the existing customers on the list, and click the Next Record button at the bottom of the Add Invoices form.

Try the above procedure with the following details:

```
AD9714    WEST       17/11/99        £140
```

then verify that indeed the information has been recorded by double-clicking the Invoices table on the Database window.

If you have any problems getting the Combo box to enter data, you may need to check the Join Properties of your database tables, as outlined on page 86. Both the Invoices and Orders tables should be linked with 'type 2' joins.

Creating a Database Menu

All the sample databases provided with Access 2000 have a starting menu system, known as a Switchboard. If you create a new database with the Database Wizard it creates a switchboard that makes it easy to navigate between the forms and reports in the new database. We shall see how to create such a switchboard from scratch, like ours below.

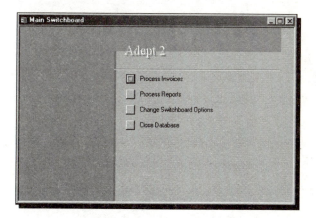

The Switchboard Manager

To start this procedure, action the **Tools**, **Database Utilities**, **Switchboard Manager** command from the main Access menu, which when used for the first time opens the following message box.

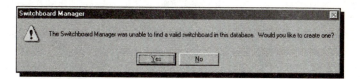

Selecting **Yes** causes a new form, with the name of Switchboard, to be placed in the Database window and opens the Switchboard Manager dialogue box shown next.

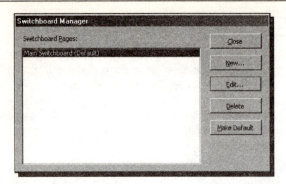

In the Switchboard Manager dialogue box, click **New**, type Invoices, and click the **OK** button to create a new menu, or switchboard, page of that name. Repeat the process and create another Reports page, as below.

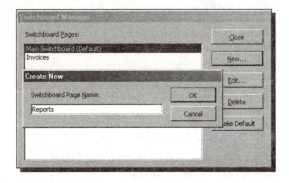

You now have three menu pages with nothing on any of them, so select the page Main Switchboard and click the **Edit** and **New** buttons in turn. Complete the Edit Switchboard Item box as shown below, where **Text** is what will appear on the menu line, **Command** is the action that will be taken and the last line holds any parameters needed.

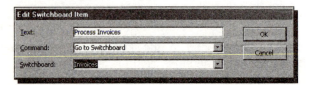

You do not have to remember anything, where there are options you can click on the down-arrow to select from them.

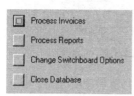

The next menu item is Process Reports which points to the Reports switchboard page. The Change Switchboard Options item opens the Switchboard Manager with the Design Application **Command**. The last item on the main switchboard is self explanatory and uses the Exit Application **Command** to close the database.

That completes the main page, so click **Close** to return to the Switchboard Manager dialogue box, select the Invoices page and click the **Edit** button. This

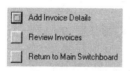

page has three items, as shown, each one being added by clicking the **New** button. The first one uses the Open Form in Add Mode **Command** to open the Add Invoices form. The second one uses the Open Form in Edit Mode **Command** to open the Customer Invoice Details form, and the last line uses the Go to Switchboard **Command** to return to the Main Switchboard.

At this stage you can place a Return to Main Switchboard item on the Reports page, so that it does not form a dead end. You can finish this menu page yourself after the next chapter.

Pressing **Close** twice should return you to the Database window, where you can finally try out your menu system by double-clicking the Switchboard form entry. Hopefully all will be well and your menu will look something like ours shown on page 117.

You can, of course, customise this form in Design view, but we suggest you go very carefully here. It is easy to corrupt the menu controls. A good idea is to make a copy of the form and play with that until you are happy. Whatever you do, please don't delete the Switchboard form from the

Database window. We did this and could not find a way of creating another one. Be warned.

An Autostart Menu

To make sure the correct switchboard page opens on your menu, ensure that the word (Default) appears at the end of the Main Switchboard name in the Switchboard Manager dialogue box, if not, then select it and click the **Make Default** button.

If you want your menu system to be displayed whenever you open the database, make the changes shown below, in the Startup dialogue box. This is opened with the **Tools**, **Startup** menu command.

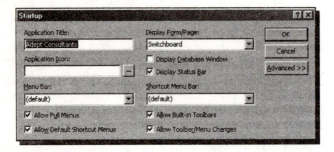

If the **Display Database Window** check box is not selected the database window will not automatically open with the database. If you need it, you will have to press the **F11** key.

Take care with some of the options in the Startup box. You should only make changes to the four lower check boxes when your database design is finalised and you have made a backup copy of it. For example, if you deselect the **Allow Full Menus** option, you will no longer be able to access Design view from your database!

Good luck with your menu system. Ours is obviously fairly simplistic and is for example only. You can make yours as complex as your own database requires.

9

Using Reports

In Access, a report is an effective way to present data in printed format. The data in a report being taken from a database table, query, or SQL statement, and the other report information is stored in the report's design. This is shown graphically in the Access Help page below.

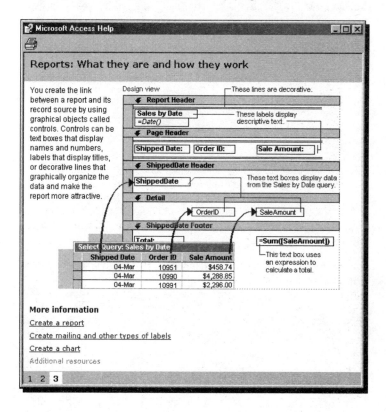

The Report Wizard

To see how easy it can be, we will use the skills gained in manipulating Access forms in Design view to produce a very quick, but acceptable, report using the Report Wizard. In our example database, **Adept 2**, we will produce a report based on the Unpaid Invoices query.

Click the Reports tab on the Database window and then press the **New** button, to open the New Report dialogue box.

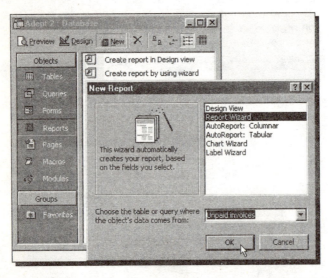

Select the Report Wizard option, and choose Unpaid Invoices as the query where the report data will come from, and press OK.

Select all the fields (except for Paid?) to appear on your report. Select the InvoiceID field as the sort field, accept all other default settings, and give it the name Unpaid Invoices Report.

The report is quickly created for you as shown on the next page, but the format is not yet quite acceptable. The problem is mainly that all the text fields are left justified while numerical fields are right justified.

Unpaid Invoices Report

Invoice No	Amount	Name	Contact	Phone
AD9701	£120.84	VORTEX Co. Ltd	Brian Storm	01776-223344
AD9703	£99.32	BARROWS Associates	Mandy Brown	01554-664422
AD9704	£55.98	STONEAGE Ltd	Mike Irons	01765-234567
AD9705	£180.22	PARKWAY Gravel	James Stone	01534-987654
AD9706	£68.52	WESTWOOD Ltd	Mary Slim	01234-667765
AD9707	£111.56	GLOWORM Ltd	Peter Summers	01432-746523
AD9709	£35.87	WORMGLAZE Ltd	Richard Glazer	01123-654321
AD9710	£58.95	EALING Engines Design	Trevor Miles	01336-010107
AD9711	£290.00	HIRE Service Equipment	Nicole Webb	01875-658822
AD9712	£160.00	EUROBASE Co. Ltd	Sarah Star	01736-098765
AD9713	£135.00	AVON Construction	John Waters	01657-113355

What we need to do is display it in Design view so that we can change the position of the numeric fields. To do this, select the report in the Database window and click the Design icon on the Toolbar which displays the underlying format of the report as follows:

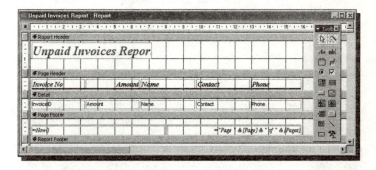

Use the mouse to lengthen the title label, then move the Amount data box to the left, and right justify the text in the Amount label and data boxes and make them smaller, as shown on the next page.

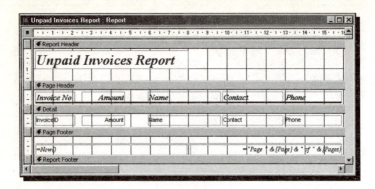

The corresponding report now prints as follows:

Unpaid Invoices Report

Invoice No	Amount	Name	Contact	Phone
AD 9701	£120.84	VORTEX Co. Ltd	Brian Storm	01776-223344
AD 9703	£99.32	BARROWS Associates	Mandy Brown	01554-664422
AD 9704	£55.98	STONEAGE Ltd	Mike Irons	01765-234567
AD 9705	£180.22	PARKWAY Gravel	James Stone	01534-987654
AD 9706	£68.52	WESTWOOD Ltd	Mary Slim	01234-667755
AD 9707	£111.56	GLOWORM Ltd	Peter Summers	01432-746523
AD 9709	£35.87	WORMGLAZE Ltd	Richard Glazer	01123-654321
AD 9710	£58.95	EALING Engines Design	Trevor Miles	01336-010107
AD 9711	£290.00	HIRE Service Equipment	Nicole Webb	01875-558822
AD 9712	£150.00	EUROBASE Co. Ltd	Sarah Star	01736-098765
AD 9713	£135.00	AVON Construction	John Waters	01657-113355

This layout is obviously far more acceptable than that of the original report created by the Report Wizard. It does not take much tweaking to get good results, and of course you only need to do this once, as long as you save your changes. The next time you double-click the name of this report in the Database window, it will be produced again with the most up-to-date data.

Types of Access Reports

In Design view you can, if you have the skill and time, create reports completely on your own. Initially we are sure most people will be happy using one of the following Wizards to create their reports, and then spend a few minutes (hopefully not hours) getting the final result.

Report Wizard - Automatically creates reports based on fields and options you select.

Autoreport: Columnar - Automatically produces a columnar report.

Autoreport: Tabular - Automatically produces a tabular report.

Chart Wizard - creates a report with a chart.

Label Wizard - creates a report formatted for you to print on mailing labels.

With the AutoReport options above, you select one record source, such as a table or query and the Wizard then uses all the fields from that source and applies the last autoformat you used to the report. With the Chart Wizard, however, you can select fields from more than one table or query source.

Report Views

With Access 2000 there are three possible screen views of a

report accessed by clicking the down-arrow next to the View toolbar button, shown here. **Print Preview** shows the report on the screen as it will be printed with all its data. In **Design View** you change the layout and content of a report. **Layout Preview** is only available from Design view, and shows the report layout with only a small sample of data.

Help on Report Building

The reporting section of Access 2000 is very powerful and we only have space to give a flavour of it here. We suggest you spend several hours at least in the Help section, accessed as usual with the **F1** key.

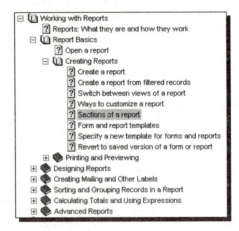

Some of the sections are graphical, very detailed and very easy to understand, as in the example shown here.

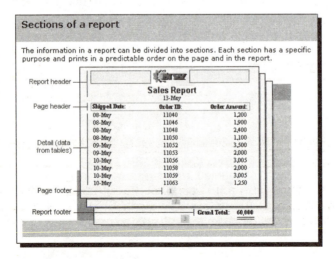

The Northwind Database

The other main source of inspiration on reports, and other database components, is the Northwind sample database packaged with Access and introduced here on page 34.

Open this database and have a look through the reports that are in it (14 in our case, but you may have a different version). We have printed out a 'cut down' sample from the Employee Sales by Country report below, and show it in Design view on the next page, so that you can compare them and get some idea how the final report is made up.

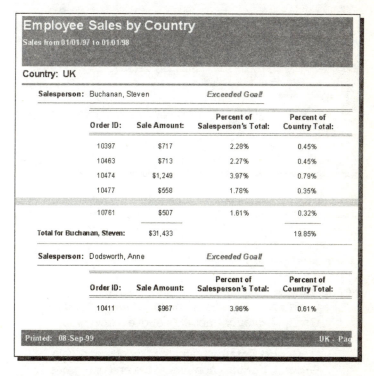

This report has two grouping selections, the first based on the Country, and the second giving details of the sales persons in that country.

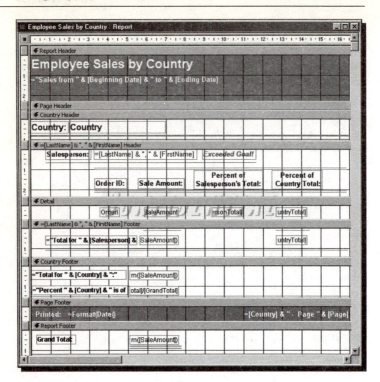

There are nine bands shown above in this report and what is shown in each band of the final report depends on the controls (mainly Labels and Text Boxes) placed on it. The function of each band and where its output appears is shown below:

Report Header - appears at the start of a report
    Page Header - appears at the top of each report page
        Group 1 Header - appears above a new group
        Group 2 Header - appears above a new group
            Report Detail - the main body of report data
        Group 2 Footer - appears at the end of a group
        Group 1 Footer - appears at the end of a group
    Page Footer - appears at the bottom of each page
Report Footer - appears at the end of a report.

Sorting and Grouping Records

In the previous example there were two report groups, but you can sort and group on up to 10 fields or expressions in a

report. You control this with the report open in Design view, by clicking the Sorting And Grouping button on the toolbar to open the Sorting And Grouping dialogue box, shown below.

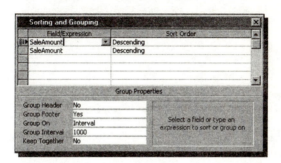

Sorting Records

In the first row of the **Field/Expression** column, select a field name from the drop-down list, or type an expression. The field or expression in this first row is the first sorting level. The second row is the second sorting level, etc. By default Access sets the **Sort Order** to Ascending which sorts from A to Z or 0 to 9. To change the sort order, select Descending from the Sort Order drop-down list.

Grouping Records

In the Sorting And Grouping dialogue box, click the field whose group properties you want to set. You must set either Group Header or Group Footer to Yes in order to create a group level and set the other grouping properties.

Group Header	Adds or removes a group header for the field or expression.
Group Footer	Adds or removes a group footer for the field or expression.

Group On	Specifies how you want the values grouped. The options depend on the data type of the field. If you group on an expression, all the data type options become available.
Group Interval	Specifies any interval that is valid for the values in the field or expression you are grouping on.
Keep Together	Specifies whether all or only part of a group is printed on the same page.

Creating a Calculated Control

It is often very useful to have a report calculate values from the data extracted from the database, such as totals, averages, percentages, etc. To describe how to do this, we will place a total value on the Unpaid Invoices Report we designed at the beginning of the chapter.

Open the Unpaid Invoices Report of the **Adept 2** database in Design view as usual and drag the Report Footer down to make room for the new controls. Select the grey line in the Page Footer band, by clicking it, and copy and paste it into the new space. Click the Text Box tool in the toolbox and 'drag' a new box about the same size as and below the Amount control in the Detail band, as shown below.

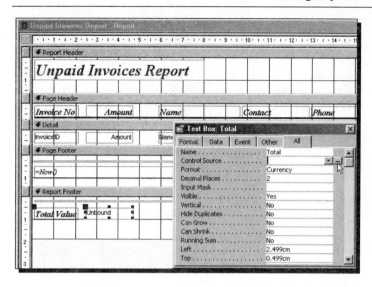

Type 'Total Value' in the Label that is placed to the left of the Text Box, and re-size the boxes as shown above.

 We must now enter the Expression into the Text box to carry out the required calculation. Make sure the Text Box control is selected, click the Properties button on the toolbar to display the control's property sheet, as shown above. Type the new control name 'Total' in the Name property box and click the Build button ••• next to the Control-Source property box. This opens the Expression Builder, shown here.

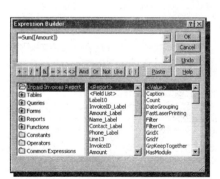

In fact with a text box, you can type the expression directly into it, but we wanted to introduce the Expression Builder! Click **Help** to read about this feature.

The expression you need to total the Amount field is:

```
=Sum([amount])
```

Either type this into the Expression Builder, or experiment with the builder until you have this expression in the top window, and then press **OK** to place the expression in the properties sheet. Clicking the **Print Preview** toolbar button should now show the following result.

Unpaid Invoices Report

Invoice No	Amount	Name	Contact	Phone
AD 9701	£120.84	VORTEX Co. Ltd	Brian Storm	01776-223344
AD 9703	£99.32	BARROWS Associates	Mandy Brown	01554-664422
AD 9704	£55.98	STONEAGE Ltd	Mike Irons	01765-234567
AD 9705	£180.22	PARKWAY Gravel	James Stone	01534-987654
AD 9706	£68.52	WESTWOOD Ltd	Mary Slim	01234-667755
AD 9707	£111.56	GLOWORM Ltd	Peter Summers	01432-746523
AD 9709	£35.87	WORMGLAZE Ltd	Richard Glazer	01123-654321
AD 9710	£58.95	EALING Engines Design	Trevor Miles	01336-010107
AD 9711	£290.00	HIRE Service Equipment	Nicole Webb	01875-558822
AD 9712	£150.00	EUROBASE Co. Ltd	Sarah Star	01736-098765
AD 9713	£135.00	AVON Construction	John Waters	01657-113355

Total Value £1,306.26

In a calculated control you should always start each expression with the = operator as can be seen on the next page where we list the other arithmetic expressions you can use in an Access database report or form.

It is usually easier to type the expression straight into a text box, or a property box, and don't forget that if you need more room to type the expression in the box, the <Shift+F2> keystroke combination will open the Zoom box for you.

Arithmetic Expressions

Expression	*Description*
=Avg([Field])	Uses the Avg function to display the average of the values of the 'Field' control.
=Count([Field])	Uses the Count function to display the number of records in the 'Field' control.
=Sum([Field])	Uses the Sum function to display the sum of the values of the 'Field' control.
=Sum([Field1]*[Field2])	Uses the Sum function to display the sum of the product of the values of the 'Field1' and 'Field2' controls.
=[Sales]/Sum([Sales])	Displays the percentage of sales, determined by dividing the value of the Sales control by the sum of all the values of the Sales control. The control's Format property must be set to Percent for this to work.

Access has quite an extensive list of expressions that can be used in tables and forms. Amongst other things, these can be used to handle text, numbers, dates, page numbers and control values.

To find out more on these, open the Help system, type 'expressions' in the **Contents** box, and select the 'Examples of Expressions' topic from the very long list produced.

All that remains to be done now is to add a menu item to the Reports page of the Switchboard form. We will leave that for you to do. In a real database it would be useful to have every report listed on this menu page.

Printing a Report

Printing a report to paper in Access is just the same as printing from any other Microsoft Windows application. If necessary, first use the **File**, **Page Setup** command to set the paper size, source, orientation and margin settings. With the report, either open, or selected in the Database window, click the Print toolbar button to use the current printer settings.

If you want to change the printer settings, you should use the **File**, **Print** command, or <Ctrl+P>, to open the Print dialogue box (shown on page 55), make the changes you want, and then click the **OK** button to start the printing operation.

10

Masking and Filtering Data

In this chapter we discuss two aspects of working with data; masking and filtering. The first is useful for restricting data input into an Access field, such as a postcode or a telephone number, to a given data mask so as to eliminate input errors. The second is invaluable if you are thinking of importing data into Access either from a flat-file database or spreadsheet, or exporting data from Access into another Windows package, such as Microsoft Word or Excel.

The Input Mask Property

You can use the Input Mask property to make data entry easier and control the values you enter in a text box. For example, you could create an input mask for a Post Code field that shows you exactly how to enter a new postcode.

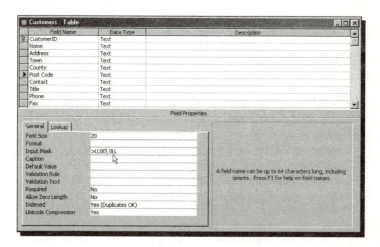

To see an input mask, open the **Adept 2** database, select the Customers table, press the Design View button, and select the Post Code field. The input mask appears in the Field Properties box, shown on the previous page.

The Input Mask property can contain up to three sections separated by semicolons (;). Within each section a certain number of characters are allowed. These characters and their description are listed below.

Character	*Description*
0	Signifies a digit (0 to 9); entry required. The plus (+) and minus (-) signs are not allowed.
9	Signifies a digit or space; entry not required. The plus and minus signs are not allowed.
#	Signifies a digit or space; entry not required, spaces are displayed as blanks while in Edit mode, but blanks are removed when data is saved. The plus and minus signs are allowed.
L	Signifies a letter (A to Z); entry required.
?	Signifies a letter (A to Z); entry optional.
A	Signifies a letter or digit; entry required.
a	Signifies a letter or digit; entry optional.
&	Signifies any character or a space; entry required.
C	Signifies any character or a space; entry optional.
. , : ; - /	Signifies a decimal placeholder and thousand, date, and time separators. (The actual character used depends on the settings in the Regional Settings section of the Windows Control Panel).
<	Causes all characters to be converted to lowercase.

> Causes all characters to be converted to uppercase.

! Causes the input mask to display from right to left, rather than from left to right, when characters on the left side of the input mask are optional. Characters typed into the mask always fill it from left to right. You can include the exclamation point anywhere in the input mask.

\ Causes the character that follows to be displayed as the literal character (for example, \A is displayed as just A).

Thus, we can interpret the postcode shown in our earlier screen dump as follows:

>   Convert all characters entered to upper case.
L   Letter (A-Z) expected; entry required.
L   Letter (A-Z) expected; entry required.
0   Digit (0-9) expected; entry required.
0   Digit (0-9) expected; entry required.
\   Cause character following backslash (in this case a space) to appear as such
0   Digit (0-9) expected; entry required.
L   Letter (A-Z) expected; entry required.
L   Letter (A-Z) expected; entry required.

However, this postcode (two letters followed by two numbers, then a space followed by one number, then two letters, will not be adequate for all the variations of postcode encountered in the UK.

For example, some codes have only one number following the first two letters, like CB1 2PU, others particularly in London have only one leading letter, like N1 0RD, while if you write to the BBC you will need the W1A 1AA code.

Thus, a postcode mask suitable for most eventualities in the UK could be:

>LAaaaaaa

To experiment with input masks, place the insertion pointer in the Post Code field of the Customers table. This causes a dotted button ··· to appear at the extreme right of the field which, when clicked, activates the Input Mask Wizard, as shown below.

Select the Post Code from the Input Mask list, and press **Next** to display the second dialogue box in which you can edit the default Input Mask. You can also type the variations of the postcode in the Try It box.

Note: If you want to create a password-entry control, use the Password input mask to set the Input Mask property to the word 'Password'. This displays an asterisk (*) on the screen for every typed character.

Only characters that you type directly in a control or combo box are affected by the input mask. Microsoft Access ignores any input masks when you import data, or run an action query.

If you define an input mask and also set the Format property for the same field, the Format property takes precedence when the data is displayed. The data in the underlying table itself is not changed, but the Format property affects the way it is displayed.

The three sections of an input mask and their description are listed below.

Section	*Description*
First	Specifies the input mask itself, for example, >LL00\ 0LL or (0000) 000000.
Second	Specifies whether Access stores the literal display characters in the table when you enter data. If you use 0 for this section, all literal display characters (for example, the parentheses in a phone number input mask) are stored with the value; if you enter 1 or leave this section blank, only characters typed into the control are stored.
Third	Specifies the character that Access displays for the space where you should type a character in the input mask. For this section, you can use any character; to display an empty string, use a space enclosed in quotation marks (" ").

The Input Mask Wizard will set the property for you.

Importing or Linking Data

Microsoft Access has an extensive help topic on importing and linking data created in other programs. Below we present the most important parts of this information so as to make it easy for you to follow.

Access can import or link table data from other Access databases (versions 2.0, 7.0/95, 8/97 and 9/2000), as well as data from other programs, such as Excel, dBASE, FoxPro, or Paradox. You can also import or link (read-only) HTML tables and lists, which can reside on your local PC, a network, or an Internet server.

Importing data creates a copy of the information in a new table in your current Access database; the source table or file is not altered. Linking data allows you to read and update data in the external data source without importing; the external data source's format is not altered so that you can continue to use the file with the program that created it originally, and you can also add, delete, or edit such data using Access.

In general, you import or link information depending on the imposed situation, as follows:

Imposed Situation	*Method to Adopt*
Inserted data needs to be updated in Access as changes are made to the data in the source file, or Source file will always be available and you want to minimise the size of the Access data file.	Link
Inserted information might need to be updated but source file might not be always accessible, or Access data file needs to be edited without having these changes reflected in the source file.	Import

If you have data in any of the following programs or formats, you can either import or link such files.

Data Source	Version or Format
Excel spreadsheets	3, 4, 5, 7/95, 8/97, 9/2000
Lotus 1-2-3 spreadsheets	.wks, .wk1, .wk3, & .wk4
dBASE	III, III+, IV, & 5
MS Visual FoxPro	2.x, 3.0, 5.0, 6.x (import)
Paradox	3.x, 4.x, & 5.0
Delimited text files	All character sets
Fixed-width text files	All character sets
HTML	1.0 (if a list), 2.0, 3.x (if a table or list)

If you have a program which can export, convert, or save its data in one of these formats, you can import that data as well.

Access uses different icons to represent linked tables and tables that are stored in the current database, as shown here. The icon that represents a linked table remains in the Database window along with tables in the current database, so you can open the table whenever you want.

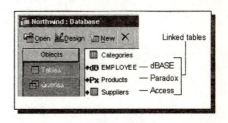

Access displays a different icon for tables from each type of source database. If you delete the icon for a linked table, you delete the link to the table, but not the external table itself.

When importing data, you cannot append it to existing tables (except when importing spreadsheet or text files). However, once you have imported a table, you can use an append query to add its data to another table.

Linked and Embedded Images

Images can be placed in object frames on Access forms or reports, as shown with one of our forms below. In this example the embedded banner image at the top, which displays with every record, was simply pasted into an Image control frame in Design mode.

The main linked image on the form is different for every record so is bound to the underlying table field, and is placed in a Bound Object frame. To enter a new linked image in **Form View** mode, right-click its field, select **Insert Object**, select **Create from File**, type in the **File** name, or use the **Browse**

button, select the **Link** check box, as shown above, and press **OK**. As long as you do not move the linked source file, the image will show whenever the record is viewed.

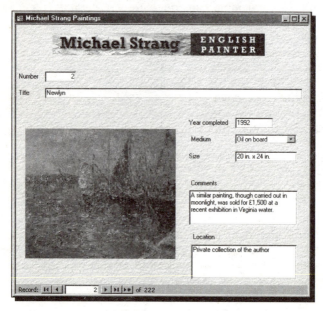

11

Access and the Internet

Microsoft has tried to integrate Access 2000 with the Internet and the Web, providing support in several ways:

- Access tables, forms, queries, and reports can contain hypertext links to objects on the Web, or elsewhere.

- You can access the Web from within a database.

- You can save tables, forms, queries, and reports as HTML pages readable by Web browsers.

- You can create 'live' Web pages based on data contained in a database.

The first two of these let you view other Internet files from your database, while the last two makes it possible for your data to be available to the outside world.

Using Hypertext Links

Hypertext links are elements on a Web page that you can click with your mouse, to jump to another Web document. You are actually fetching another file to your PC, and the link is an address that uniquely identifies the location of the target file, wherever it may be. This address is known as a Uniform Resource Locator (URL for short).

Access incorporates hypertext in two ways.

- Through hypertext fields in tables containing links, which you can click to retrieve the linked target.

- Through hyperlinks inserted as elements within forms and reports.

For an Internet link to work you must obviously have access to the Internet from your PC. The targets of these links, however, need not be Internet pages but can be other files on a hard disc drive, or objects within a database.

Creating a Hyperlink Field

To create a Hyperlink field in an open table, select Design view, create the new field, click the Data Type drop-down arrow, and then click Hyperlink. Make sure you save the changes to the table, by clicking the Save toolbar button.

Inserting a Hyperlink

 You use the Insert Hyperlink button to create a hyperlink within a Hyperlink field or as hypertext within a form or report. A hyperlink, in Access, consists of the text that the user sees that describes the link, the URL of the link's target, and a ScreenTip that appears whenever the pointer passes over the link.

Within a Hyperlink field or while editing a form or report in Design view, click the Insert Hyperlink button on the toolbar to open the Insert Hyperlink dialogue box, shown below.

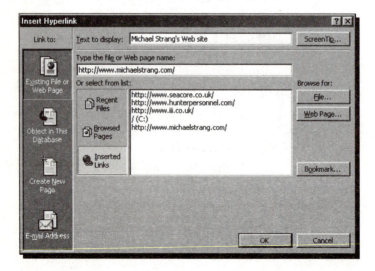

If necessary, click **E_x_isting File or Web Page** on the 'Link to' bar and enter the hyperlink text in the **T_e_xt to display** box. Specify the linked document by either: typing its filename or URL in the **Type the fil_e_ or Web page name** box, or choosing from **Or select from list** box. With the latter you have the choice of **Re_c_ent Files**, **_B_rowsed Pages**, or **_I_nserted Links**. Hopefully there won't be too many embarrassing references in these lists, big brother is watching you these days!

Click **Screen Tip** to create a Screen Tip that will be displayed whenever the mouse pointer moves over the hyperlink.

Clicking **OK** will place the link onto your Access object. Our example above placed the link on a form shown below in both Design and Form views.

Navigating the Internet from Access

Once you click a hyperlink it is activated and, as long as you are connected to the Internet, Access displays the Web toolbar which contains buttons that help you navigate the

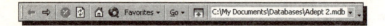

Web, as shown above. In fact, if you are using Explorer 5 as your browser, its window replaces that of Access while you are viewing a live Web page. As you progress through a series of links, the toolbar displays buttons that allow you to go forward and backward through the sequence. It also includes buttons to access a list of 'favorite' Web pages or a 'start', or Home, page. So far these are all standard browser buttons, the exception being the 'Show only Web toolbar'

 button, shown here, whose very useful toggle function is self explanatory. It gives you more screen space by closing the other Access toolbars.

Creating Access Web Pages

Most Web pages are written in HTML (Hypertext Markup Language), which can be used by Web browsers on any operating system, such as Windows, Macintosh, and UNIX.

Static Web Pages

Access allows you to export reports, forms, and tables in HTML format. Once you export these database objects, you can publish them as Web pages. These are called static pages because once formed they stand alone from the original database and cannot change when it changes.

To do this, open a table, query, form, or report in your database, use the **File**, **Export** menu command, click the **Save in** drop-down arrow, select a location for the file and enter a **File name** for the Web page. Click the **Save as type** drop-down arrow, and select HTML Documents from the list of save options. Click **Save All**. Enter the name of the HTML template to use for this Web page (if they exist these are usually stored in the '\Program Files\Microsoft Office\ Templates\Access' folder) and click **OK**.

A new Web page should have been produced. On it, tables, queries, and forms will all appear as HTML tables, but a report appears in HTML format with the same layout it had in Access.

Active Server Pages

If your Web site accesses your database, and needs to show current data, you can now use dynamic pages. Access 2000 provides two ways of exporting reports, forms, and tables in a dynamic Web page format. The more established method is with Active Server Pages, ASP for short. When an .asp file is requested by a Web browser it attempts to retrieve the most current data from its source database. This data is then formatted depending on the layout embedded in the ASP page.

Typical examples common on the Internet are sites that provide continuously updated share price information. They have a central database on their server and the information you receive in your browser is provided on ASP pages, with the file suffix .asp.

Requirements for ASP

To create an ASP file with Access 2000, you need to know the name of the current database, the user name and password to connect to the database, and the URL of the Web server that will store the ASP file. This server must be running Microsoft Active Server 3.0 or later, have the ActiveX Server component installed, along with the Microsoft Access Desktop Driver, and must have access privileges to the database. In other words, this cannot be done lightly and it needs the full co-operation of the Web site administration.

Exporting to an ASP File

In the Database window, click the database object you want to export, action the **File**, **Export** menu command. Click the **Save as type** drop-down arrow, and select Microsoft Active

Server Pages. Click the **Save in** drop-down arrow, and then select the location where you want to save the file. Click **Save**. Enter the name of the HTML template (if one exists), and the name of the database file that contains the data you want the Web server to access. Enter the user name you want the Web server to use to connect to the database and the password you want the Web server to use to log on to the database. Finally enter the Web server URL and click **OK**.

Data Access Pages

Data access pages are written in dynamic HTML or DHTML, which allow dynamic objects in a Web page. They are designed to be viewed by a Web browser but are bound directly to the data in the database. They are shown in an object group in the Database window and can be used like normal Access forms but are, in fact, stored as external files. You can also format data access pages, using many of the same tools you use when creating Access forms.

As long as you have Internet Explorer 5.0 or later installed on your system, you can create a data access page within Access 2000 in Design view, or using a wizard.

Using the Page Wizard

In the Database window, click Pages on the Objects bar, and double-click the 'Create data access page by using wizard' option. Select the table and fields that you want to appear in the data access page and click **Next** to continue. Select any fields you want to act as group levels in the Web page and click **Next** to continue. Select the fields to sort the records in the page by, and click **Next** to continue. Enter a title for the data access page and indicate whether you want to **Open the page** in Access or to modify its design in Design view, then click the **Finish** button.

You can also create a data access page with the **File**, **Export** menu command, by selecting Microsoft Access Data Access Page as the file type.

Alternatively, you can create a data access page by clicking the New button on the Database window toolbar, clicking Design View, and choosing the table or query you want placed in the data access page.

Viewing a Data Access Page

You can open a data access page from within the database itself or from your Web browser. In the Database window, click Pages on the Objects bar and double-click the data access page you want to view. The page opens in a separate window.

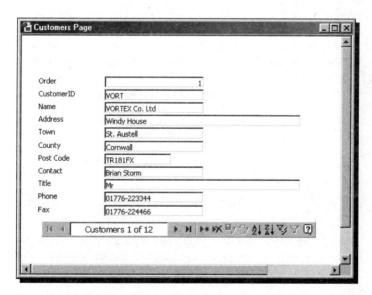

We created a data access page from the Customers table of the **Adept 2** database, as shown above.

The **File**, **Web Page Preview** menu command will start your Web browser and load a selected data access page, whose data you can then view and edit as you like.

Data access pages contain a navigation bar, as shown below, to help you retrieve records, filter and sort the data, or search for specific values.

Clicking the Help button opens the Microsoft Access Data Pages Help system if you need more detailed assistance.

Adding a Theme to a Page

Access 2000 has a collection of Web page themes that give you a variety of standard page designs. These control the background, fonts, and colours used in the Web page.

With the data access page in Design view, use the **Format**, **Theme** menu command, select the theme you want to apply and select the theme options you want.

****

Well that's it. We hope you have enjoyed reading this as much as we have enjoyed writing it. A glossary is included next, for reference, and in case you have trouble with any jargon that may have crept in.

12

Glossary of Terms

ActiveX
A set of technologies that enables software components to interact with one another in a networked environment, regardless of the language in which the components were created.

Add-in
A mini-program which runs in conjunction with another and enhances its functionality.

Address
A unique number or name that identifies a specific computer or user on a network.

Anonymous FTP
Anonymous FTP allows you to connect to a remote computer and transfer public files back to your local computer without the need to have a user ID and password.

Application
Software (program) designed to carry out certain activity, such as word processing, or data management.

Applet
A program that can be downloaded over a network and launched on the user's computer.

Archie
Archie is an Internet service that allows you to locate files that can be downloaded via FTP.

ASP	Active Server Page. File format used for dynamic Web pages that get their data from a server based database.
Association	An identification of a filename extension to a program. This lets Windows open the program when its files are selected.
ASCII	A binary code representation of a character set. The name stands for 'American Standard Code for Information Interchange'.
Authoring	The process of creating web documents or software.
AVI	Audio Video Interleaved. A Windows multimedia file format for sound and moving pictures.
Backbone	The main transmission lines of the Internet, running at over 45Mbps.
Backup	To make a back-up copy of a file or a disc for safekeeping.
Bandwidth	The range of transmission frequencies a network can use. The greater the bandwidth the more information that can be transferred over a network.
Banner	An advertising graphic shown on a Web page.
BASIC	Beginner's All-purpose Symbolic Instruction Code - a high-level programming language.
BBS	Bulletin Board System, a computer equipped with software and telecoms links that allow it to act as an information host for remote computer systems.

Beta test	A test of software that is still under development, by people actually using the software.
BinHex	A file conversion format that converts binary files to ASCII text files.
Bitmap	A technique for managing the image displayed on a computer screen.
Bookmark	A marker inserted at a specific point in a document to which the user may wish to return for later reference.
Bound control	A control on a database form, report or data access page that is tied to a field in an underlying table or query.
Browse	A button in some Windows dialogue boxes that lets you view a list of files and folders before you make a selection.
Browser	A program, like the Internet Explorer, that lets you view Web pages.
Bug	An error in coding or logic that causes a program to malfunction.
Button	A graphic element in a dialogue box or toolbar that performs a specified function.
Cache	An area of memory, or disc space, reserved for data, which speeds up downloading.
Card	A removable printed-circuit board that is plugged into a computer expansion slot.
CD-ROM	Compact Disc - Read Only Memory; an optical disc which information may be read from but not written to.

CGI	Common Gateway Interface - a convention for servers to communicate with local applications and allow users to provide information to scripts attached to web pages, usually through forms.
Cgi-bin	The most common name of a directory on a web server in which CGI programs are stored.
Chart	A graphical view of data that is used to visually display trends, patterns, and comparisons.
Click	To press and release a mouse button once without moving the mouse.
Client	A computer that has access to services over a computer network. The computer providing the services is a server.
Client application	A Windows application that can accept linked, or embedded, objects.
Clipboard	A temporary storage area of memory, where text and graphics are stored with the Windows cut and copy actions.
Command	An instruction given to a computer to carry out a particular action.
Compressed file	One that is compacted to save server space and reduce transfer times. Typical file extensions for compressed files include .zip (DOS/Windows) and .tar (UNIX).
Configuration	A general purpose term referring to the way you have your computer set up.

Controls	Objects on a form, report, or data access page that display data, perform actions, or are used for decoration.
Cookies	Files stored on your hard drive by your Web browser that hold information for it to use.
CPU	The Central Processing Unit; the main chip that executes all instructions entered into a computer.
Cyberspace	Originated by William Gibson in his novel 'Neuromancer', now used to describe the Internet and the other computer networks.
Data access page	A Web page, created by Access, that has a connection to a database; you can view, add, edit, and manipulate the data in this page.
Database	A collection of data related to a particular topic or purpose.
DBMS	Database management system - A software interface between the database and the user.
Dial-up Connection	A popular form of Net connection for the home user, over standard telephone lines.
Direct Connection	A permanent connection between your computer system and the Internet.
Default	The command, device or option automatically chosen.
Desktop	The Windows screen working background, on which you place icons, folders, etc.

Device driver	A special file that must be loaded into memory for Windows to be able to address a specific procedure or hardware device.
Device name	A logical name used by DOS to identify a device, such as LPT1 or COM1 for the parallel or serial printer.
Dialogue box	A window displayed on the screen to allow the user to enter information.
Directory	An area on disc where information relating to a group of files is kept. Also known as a folder.
Disc	A device on which you can store programs and data.
Disconnect	To detach a drive, port or computer from a shared device, or to break an Internet connection.
Document	A file produced by an application program. When used in reference to the Web, a document is any file containing text, media or hyperlinks that can be transferred from an HTTP server to a browser.
Domain	A group of devices, servers and computers on a network.
Domain Name	The name of an Internet site, for example www.michaelstrang.com, which allows you to reference Internet sites without knowing their true numerical address.
DOS	Disc Operating System. A collection of small specialised programs that allow interaction between user and computer.

Double-click	To quickly press and release a mouse button twice.
Download	To transfer to your computer a file, or data, from another computer.
DPI	Dots Per Inch - a resolution standard for laser printers.
Drag	To move an object on the screen by pressing and holding down the left mouse button while moving the mouse.
Drive name	The letter followed by a colon which identifies a floppy or hard disc drive.
EISA	Extended Industry Standard Architecture, for construction of PCs with the Intel 32-bit micro-processor.
Embedded object	Information in a document that is 'copied' from its source application. Selecting the object opens the creating application from within the document.
Engine	Software used by search services.
E-mail	Electronic Mail - A system that allows computer users to send and receive messages electronically.
Ethernet	A very common method of networking computers in a LAN.
FAQ	Frequently Asked Questions - A common feature on the Internet, FAQs are files of answers to commonly asked questions.
FAT	The File Allocation Table. An area on disc where information is kept on which part of the disc a file is located.

File extension	The suffix following the period in a filename. Windows uses this to identify the source application program. For example .mdb indicates an Access file.
Filename	The name given to a file. In Windows 95 and above this can be up to 256 characters long.
Filter	A set of criteria that is applied to data to show a subset of the data.
Firewall	Security measures designed to protect a networked system from unauthorised access.
Floppy disc	A removable disc on which information can be stored magnetically.
Folder	An area used to store a group of files, usually with a common link.
Font	A graphic design representing a set of characters, numbers and symbols.
Freeware	Software that is available for downloading and unlimited use without charge.
FTP	File Transfer Protocol. The procedure for connecting to a remote computer and transferring files.
Function key	One of the series of 10 or 12 keys marked with the letter F and a numeral, used for specific operations.
Gateway	A computer system that allows otherwise incompatible networks to communicate with each other.

GIF	Graphics Interchange Format, a common standard for images on the Web.
Graphic	A picture or illustration, also called an image. Formats include GIF, JPEG, BMP, PCX, and TIFF.
Graphics card	A device that controls the display on the monitor and other allied functions.
GUI	A Graphic User Interface, such as Windows 98, the software front-end meant to provide an attractive and easy to use interface.
Hard copy	Output on paper.
Hard disc	A device built into the computer for holding programs and data.
Hardware	The equipment that makes up a computer system, excluding the programs or software.
Help	A Windows system that gives you instructions and additional information on using a program.
Helper application	A program allowing you to view multimedia files that your web browser cannot handle internally.
Hit	A single request from a web browser for a single item from a web server.
Home page	The document displayed when you first open your Web browser, or the first document you come to at a Web site.
Host	Computer connected directly to the Internet that provides services to other local and/or remote computers.

Hotlist	A list of frequently used Web locations and URL addresses.
Host	A computer acting as an information or communications server.
HTML	HyperText Markup Language, the format used in documents on the Web.
HTML editor	Authoring tool which assists with the creation of HTML pages.
HTTP	HyperText Transport Protocol, the system used to link and transfer hypertext documents on the Web.
Hyperlink	A segment of text, or an image, that refers to another document on the Web, an Intranet or your PC.
Hypermedia	Hypertext extended to include linked multimedia.
Hypertext	A system that allows documents to be cross-linked so that the reader can explore related links, or documents, by clicking on a highlighted symbol.
Icon	A small graphic image that represents a function or object. Clicking on an icon produces an action.
Image	See graphic.
Insertion point	A flashing bar that shows where typed text will be entered into a document.
Interface	A device that allows you to connect a computer to its peripherals.
Internet	The global system of computer networks.

Intranet	A private network inside an organisation using the same kind of software as the Internet.
ISA	Industry Standard Architecture; a standard for internal connections in PCs.
ISDN	Integrated Services Digital Network, a telecom standard using digital transmission technology to support voice, video and data communications applications over regular telephone lines.
IP	Internet Protocol - The rules that provide basic Internet functions.
IP Address	Internet Protocol Address - every computer on the Internet has a unique identifying number.
ISP	Internet Service Provider - A company that offers access to the Internet.
Java	An object-oriented programming language created by Sun Microsystems for developing applications and applets that are capable of running on any computer, regardless of the operating system.
JPEG /JPG	Joint Photographic Experts Group, a popular cross-platform format for image files. JPEG is best suited for true colour original images.
Kilobyte	(KB); 1024 bytes of information or storage space.
LAN	Local Area Network - High-speed, privately-owned network covering a

	limited geographical area, such as an office or a building.
Laptop	A portable computer small enough to sit on your lap.
LCD	Liquid Crystal Display.
Links	The hypertext connections between Web pages.
Local	A resource that is located on your computer, not linked to it over a network.
Location	An Internet address.
Log on	To gain access to a network.
MCI	Media Control Interface - a standard for files and multimedia devices.
Megabyte	MB); 1024 kilobytes of information or storage space.
Megahertz	(MHz); Speed of processor in millions of cycles per second.
Memory	Part of computer consisting of storage elements organised into addressable locations that can hold data and instructions.
Menu	A list of available options in an application.
Menu bar	The horizontal bar that lists the names of menus.
MIDI	Musical Instrument Digital Interface - enables devices to transmit and receive sound and music messages.
MIME	Multipurpose Internet Mail Extensions, a messaging standard that allows Internet users to exchange

e-mail messages enhanced with graphics, video and voice.

MIPS — Million Instructions Per Second; measures speed of a system.

Modem — Short for Modulator-demodulator devices. An electronic device that lets computers communicate electronically.

Monitor — The display device connected to your PC, also called a screen.

Mouse — A device used to manipulate a pointer around your display and activate processes by pressing buttons.

MPEG — Motion Picture Experts Group - a video file format offering excellent quality in a relatively small file.

MS-DOS — Microsoft's implementation of the Disc Operating System for PCs.

Multimedia — The use of photographs, music and sound and movie images in a presentation.

Multi-tasking — Performing more than one operation at the same time.

Network — Two or more computers connected together to share resources.

Network server — Central computer which stores files for several linked computers.

Node — Any single computer connected to a network.

ODBC — Open DataBase Connectivity - A standard protocol for accessing information in a SQL database server.

OLE	Object Linking and Embedding - A technology for transferring and sharing information among software applications.
Online	Having access to the Internet.
On-line Service	Services such as America On-line and CompuServe that provide content to subscribers and usually connections to the Internet.
Operating system	Software that runs a computer.
Page	An HTML document, or Web site.
Password	A unique character string used to gain access to a network, program, or mailbox.
PATH	The location of a file in the directory tree.
Peripheral	Any device attached to a PC.
Perl	A popular language for programming CGI applications.
PIF file	Program information file - gives information to Windows about an MS-DOS application.
Pixel	A picture element on screen; the smallest element that can be independently assigned colour and intensity.
Plug-and-play	Hardware which can be plugged into a PC and be used immediately without configuration.
POP	Post Office Protocol - a method of storing and returning e-mail.
Port	The place where information goes into or out of a computer, e.g. a

	modem might be connected to the serial port.
PPP	Point-to-Point Protocol - One of two methods (see SLIP) for using special software to establish a temporary direct connection to the Internet over regular phone lines.
Print queue	A list of print jobs waiting to be sent to a printer.
Program	A set of instructions which cause a computer to perform tasks.
Protocol	A set of rules or standards that define how computers communicate with each other.
Query	The set of keywords and operators sent by a user to a search engine, or a database search request.
Queue	A list of e-mail messages waiting to be sent over the Internet.
RAM	Random Access Memory. The computer's volatile memory. Data held in it is lost when power is switched off.
Real mode	MS-DOS mode, typically used to run programs, such as MS-DOS games, that will not run under Windows.
Resource	A directory, or printer, that can be shared over a network.
Robot	A Web agent that visits sites, by requesting documents from them, for the purposes of indexing for search engines. Also known as Wanderers, Crawlers, or Spiders.
ROM	Read Only Memory. A PC's non-volatile memory. Data is written

	into this memory at manufacture and is not affected by power loss.
Scroll bar	A bar that appears at the right side or bottom edge of a window.
Search	Submit a query to a search engine.
Search engine	A program that helps users find information across the Internet.
Serial interface	An interface that transfers data as individual bits.
Server	A computer system that manages and delivers information for client computers.
Shared resource	Any device, program or file that is available to network users.
Shareware	Software that is available on public networks and bulletin boards. Users are expected to pay a nominal amount to the software developer.
Signature file	An ASCII text file, maintained within e-mail programs, that contains text for your signature.
Site	A place on the Internet. Every Web page has a location where it resides which is called its site.
SLIP	Serial Line Internet Protocol, a method of Internet connection that enables computers to use phone lines and a modem to connect to the Internet without having to connect to a host.
SMTP	Simple Mail Transfer Protocol - a protocol dictating how e-mail messages are exchanged over the Internet.

Socket	An endpoint for sending and receiving data between computers.
Software	The programs and instructions that control your PC.
Spamming	Sending the same message to a large number of mailing lists or newsgroups. Also to overload a Web page with excessive keywords in an attempt to get a better search ranking.
Spider	See robot.
Spooler	Software which handles transfer of information to a store to be used by a peripheral device.
SQL	Structured Query Language, used with relational databases.
SSL	Secure Sockets Layer, the standard transmission security protocol developed by Netscape, which has been put into the public domain.
Subscribe	To become a member of.
Surfing	The process of looking around the Internet.
SVGA	Super Video Graphics Array; it has all the VGA modes but with 256, or more, colours.
Swap file	An area of your hard disc used to store temporary operating files, also known as virtual memory.
Sysop	System Operator - A person responsible for the physical operations of a computer system or network resource.

System disc	A disc containing files to enable a PC to start up.
T1	An Internet leased line that carries up to 1.536 million bits per second (1.536Mbps).
T3	An Internet leased line that carries up to 45 million bits per second (45Mbps).
TCP/IP	Transmission Control Protocol/Internet Protocol, combined protocols that perform the transfer of data between two computers. TCP monitors and ensures the correct transfer of data. IP receives the data, breaks it up into packets, and sends it to a network within the Internet.
Telnet	A program which allows people to remotely use computers across networks.
Text file	An unformatted file of text characters saved in ASCII format.
Thread	An ongoing message-based conversation on a single subject.
TIFF	Tag Image File Format - a popular graphic image file format.
Tool	Software program used to support Web site creation and management.
Toolbar	A bar containing icons giving quick access to commands.
Toggle	To turn an action on and off with the same switch.
TrueType fonts	Fonts that can be scaled to any size and print as they show on the screen.

UNC	Universal Naming Convention - A convention for files that provides a machine independent means of locating the file that is particularly useful in Web based applications.
UNIX	Multitasking, multi-user computer operating system that is run by many computers that are connected to the Internet.
Upload/Download	The process of transferring files between computers. Files are uploaded from your computer to another and downloaded from another computer to your own.
URL	Uniform Resource Locator, the addressing system used on the Web, containing information about the method of access, the server to be accessed and the path of the file to be accessed.
Usenet	Informal network of computers that allow the posting and reading of messages in newsgroups that focus on specific topics.
User ID	The unique identifier, usually used in conjunction with a password, which identifies you on a computer.
Virtual Reality	Simulations of real or imaginary worlds, rendered on a flat two-dimensional screen but appearing three-dimensional.
Virus	A malicious program, downloaded from a web site or disc, designed to wipe out information on your computer.

W3C	The World Wide Web Consortium that is steering standards development for the Web.
WAIS	Wide Area Information Server, a Net-wide system for looking up specific information in Internet databases.
WAV	Waveform Audio (.wav) - a common audio file format for DOS/Windows computers.
Web	A network of hypertext-based multimedia information servers. Browsers are used to view any information on the Web.
Web Page	An HTML document that is accessible on the Web.
Webmaster	One whose job it is to manage a web site.
WINSOCK	A Microsoft Windows file that provides the interface to TCP/IP services.
Wizard	A Microsoft tool that asks you questions and then creates an object depending on your answers.

Index

A

Access
  screen   10
  Web pages   146
Action queries   70, 94
Active
  Server Pages   147
  window   11
Adding
  fields to queries   73
  Lookup column   53
  Office features   35
  page theme   150
  records   48
  tables   37, 64
Advanced queries   85
AND criteria   75
Answer Wizard   18
Append query   94
Application control menu   10
Arithmetic expressions   133
ASP   147
AutoForm   45
AutoNumber   43
Autostart menu   120

B

Blank database   9, 25
Bound object frame   111, 142
Buttons   10

C

Calculated fields   79, 130
Calculating query totals   82
Calendar control   113

Cells
  selecting   47
  zoom   47
Chart Wizard   104
Check box   110
Close button   10, 12
Column
  table   50
  widths   50
Combining criteria   76
Combo box   110, 114
Command button   11, 111
Control Panel   34
Controls   109
Creating
  Active Server Pages   147
  calculated fields   79
  Data access pages   148
  database   29
  forms   45, 100
  groups   33
  Hypertext links   144
  queries   57, 72
  Switchboard menu   117
  tables   37, 64
  Web pages   146
Criteria
  AND   75
  OR   76, 77
  types   75
Crosstab query   70, 90
Customising
  forms   106
  Office Assistant   22

D

Data
Access pages	148
box	107
masking/filtering	135
selecting	47
types	40

Data-definition query	70

Database
basics	25
controls	109
definition	1
elements	27
flat-file	1, 2
form	45, 99
management system	1
menu	117
on-line	36
Open	17
relationships	61
samples	34
size	1
table	27, 37
Window	10, 26, 31
Wizard	9, 29

Datasheet view	42
Delete query	94

Deleting
fields	52
records	49

Design
table	37
view	32, 39

Dialogue box	9
Dynamic HTML	148

E

Edit
command	15
Lookup list	54

relationships	63
Embedded object	142
Equi-joins	87
Expanding menus	14
Export data	141
Expressions	133

F

Field
definition	1
names	37
selecting	46

Fields
deleting	52
freeze	51
hiding	51
in queries	73
inserting	52
moving	52
renaming	52

File command	13, 15
Filename extensions	26
Filtering data	44, 135

Finding
duplicate records	67
part of date field	81
part of text field	80
records	48

Flat file	1, 2

Form
customising	106
types	103
Wizard	100, 103

Forms	27, 45, 99
Freeze fields	51
Functions in criteria	80, 82

G

Glossary	151
Groups	33

Grouping records	129

H

Hardware requirements	3
Help	
command	18
queries	98
relationships	66
reports	121, 126
Toolbar	19
Hiding fields	51
HTML	146
Hypertext	
fields	144
links	144

I

Images	142
Image command	111
Importing data	140
Inherited relationships	63
Inner joins	87
Input mask	
property	135
Wizard	138
Insert command	16
Inserting	
fields	52
Installing Access	4
Internet	143

J

Joins	61, 87, 116

L

Label	109
Label box	115
Launcher	5
Line control	112
Linking data	140, 142

Links, Hypertext	143
List box	110
Lookup	
column	53
list	54
Wizard	53

M

Macros	28
Maintenance mode	35
Make-table query	94
Manipulate columns	50
Masking data	135
Maximise button	11
Maximum	
fields in a table	2
objects in database	2
Menu	
Autostart	120
bar	10
bar options	13
database	117
expanding	14
Shortcut	17
Minimise button	11
Modules	28
Mouse pointer(s)	6
Moving fields	52

N

Navigate Internet	145
New	
database	25, 29
query	72
table	37
Northwind database	127

O

Objects	2, 27, 31
embedded	142

linked	142	**R**	
Office		RAM	3
Assistant	20	Record	
shortcut bar	9	definition of	1
On-line help	18	grouping in report	129
Opening documents	9	selecting	46
Operating system	3, 146	sorting in report	129
Option		Rectangle control	113
button	110	Redesigning a Table	39
group	109	Referential integrity	62
OR criteria	77	Relational database	1, 57
Outer joins	87	Relationships	61
		Renaming fields	39
P		Report Wizard	122
Page	28	Report	28, 121
break control	112	Help	126
theme	150	printing	134
Wizard	148	types of	125
Parameter query	70	views	125
Pass-through query	70	Restore button	11
Password control	139	Run icon	74
Post code masks	137		
Printing		**S**	
reports	134	Sample databases	34
tables	55	Screen	10
Properties	40	tip	144
		Scroll	
Q		bar	10, 12
QBE grid	70	button	10, 12
Queries	27, 67, 85	Select query	70
Query		Selecting data	46
action	94	Self-joins	87
crosstab	90	SETUP program	4
Help on	98	Shortcut menus	17
parameter	88	Software requirements	3
totals	82	Sort	
types	70	filter	44
updating	93	records in report	129
window	71	Sorting a Table	43
Wizards	67, 72	Starting Access	9

Static Web pages 146
Status bar 10, 13
Start button 4
SQL statements 70, 72
Subform 100, 112
Subreport 112
Switchboard 30
   Manager 117

T
Tab control 111
Table 27
   definition 1
   design 37, 64
   printing 55
   relationships 61
   sorting 43
   view printing 55
   Wizard 37
Text box 109
Theme, page 150
Title bar 10, 11
Toggle button 109
Toolbars 10, 12
   Database window 32
   Help 19
Tools command 16
Toolbox 108
Totals in queries 82
Types of
   criteria 75
   forms 103
   joins 61, 87
   queries 70
   relationships 61
   reports 125

U
Unbound
   Control 111

Object frame 111
Unhide columns 51
Unfreeze columns 52
Union query 70
Update
   features 36
   query 93
URL 143
Using
   Form Wizard 100, 103
   forms 45, 99
   functions in criteria 80
   help 18, 98, 126
   parameter query 88
   Query Wizard 72
   Report Wizard 122
   reports 121
   Table Wizard 37
   wildcard characters 75

V
View command 15
Viewing
   Data access pages 149
   relationships 63

W
Web pages 146
What's this? Pointer 8
Width of columns 42, 50
Wildcard characters 75
Window
   command 16
   Database 31
Wizards
   Answer 18
   Chart 104
   Database 9, 29
   Form 100, 103
   Input Mask 138

Wizards (continued)

Lookup 53

Page 148

Queries 67, 72

Report 122

Table 37

Z

Zoom 47, 132

Companion Discs

COMPANION DISCS are available for most computer books written by the same author(s) and published by BERNARD BABANI (publishing) LTD, as listed at the front of this book (except for those marked with an asterisk). These books contain many pages of file/program listings. There is no reason why you should spend hours typing them into your computer, unless you wish to do so, or need the practice.

ORDERING INSTRUCTIONS

To obtain companion discs, fill in the order form below, or a copy of it, enclose a cheque (payable to **P.R.M. Oliver**) or a postal order, and send it to the address given below. **Make sure you fill in your name and address** and specify the book number and title in your order.

Book No.	Book Name	Unit Price	Total Price
BP		£3.50	
BP		£3.50	
BP		£3.50	
Name .... Address		Sub-total	£.............
		P & P (@ 45p/disc)	£.............
		Total Due	£.............
Send to: P.R.M. Oliver, CSM, Pool, Redruth, Cornwall, TR15 3SE			

PLEASE NOTE

The author(s) are fully responsible for providing this Companion Disc service. The publishers of this book accept no responsibility for the supply, quality, or magnetic contents of the disc, or in respect of any damage, or injury that might be suffered or caused by its use.